At Issue

| Biodiversity

Other Books in the At Issue Series:

At Issue

Biodiversity

Louise I. Gerdes, Book Editor

GREENHAVEN PRESS
A part of Gale, Cengage Learning

GALE
CENGAGE Learning

Detroit • New York • San Francisco • New Haven, Conn • Waterville, Maine • London

Christine Nasso, *Publisher*
Elizabeth Des Chenes, *Managing Editor*

© 2010 Greenhaven Press, a part of Gale, Cengage Learning.

Gale and Greenhaven Press are registered trademarks used herein under license.

For more information, contact:
Greenhaven Press
27500 Drake Rd.
Farmington Hills, MI 48331-3535
Or you can visit our Internet site at gale.cengage.com

For product information and technology assistance, contact us at

Gale Customer Support, 1-800-877-4253
For permission to use material from this text or product, submit all requests online at www.cengage.com/permissions

Further permissions questions can be emailed to permissionrequest@cengage.com

Articles in Greenhaven Press anthologies are often edited for length to meet page requirements. In addition, original titles of these works are changed to clearly present the main thesis and to explicitly indicate the author's opinion. Every effort is made to ensure that Greenhaven Press accurately reflects the original intent of the authors. Every effort has been made to trace the owners of copyrighted material.

Cover Image copyright, Debra Hughes 2007. Used under license from Shutterstock.com.

LIBRARY OF CONGRESS CATALOGING-IN-PUBLICATION DATA

Biodiversity / Louise I. Gerdes, book editor.
    p. cm. -- (At issue)
Includes bibliographical references and index.
ISBN 978-0-7377-4677-8 (hardcover) -- ISBN 978-0-7377-4678-5 (pbk.)
1. Biodiversity--Juvenile literature. 2. Endangered species--Juvenile literature. I. Gerdes, Louise I., 1953-
    QH541.15.B56B566 2010
    333.95'16--dc22
                                                                2010004590

Printed in the United States of America
1 2 3 4 5 6 7 14 13 12 11 10

Contents

Introduction

The desire to conserve wildlife and habitat is not new. As early as the nineteenth century, writers such as Henry David Thoreau and naturalists such as John Muir—founder of the Sierra Club—advocated the preservation of wilderness areas. In the early 1900s, U.S. policy makers created national parks and established agencies to restore depleted wildlife. Efforts to reduce the impact of human activities on wildlife grew after the publication of Rachel Carson's 1962 book *Silent Spring*, in which she exposed the dangers of DDT and other pesticides and the risk these chemicals posed to wildlife. In 1973, Congress responded to increasing public concern about threats to wildlife with the Endangered Species Act. The United States also advanced negotiations that led to the Convention on International Trade in Endangered Species of Wild Fauna and Flora, ultimately ratified by 173 nations. The convention provided protection for some 30,000 animal and plant species.

These efforts afforded wildlife in Europe and North America some protection and led to the recovery of some endangered species. However, research on the complex relationships between biodiversity and human survival in recent decades has driven many environmental activists to demand more widespread conservation efforts.

However, population pressures—particularly in the developing world—make efforts to protect biodiversity an ongoing challenge. Economic development in these nations is necessary to provide for the needs of the people, yet many developing nations are within biodiversity hotspots—areas rich in biodiversity that face serious threats. In 1992 a global commission known as the Earth Summit created the Convention on Biological Diversity, which calls for the worldwide protection of endangered species and the establishment of parks and reserves to preserve habitat. The convention has since been adopted by 178 countries. Despite these efforts, resistance in both the developed and developing world remains, prompting some to question the strategies used to encourage conservation. Conservation efforts have thus far stressed the importance of preserving nature for its aesthetic value or out of respect for all forms of life. For some, appealing to these values is not enough to decrease biodiversity loss. Indeed, the debate over the efficacy of strategies to protect biodiversity is reflective of the overarching biodiversity debate.

In recent years, those seeking to protect biodiversity have begun to promote the economic value of wild species—the "natural capital" that some claim is essential to human survival. These concerns have led conservationists such as Stanford University ecologist Gretchen C. Daily to change their approach. "Appealing to moral sense isn't enough anymore," Daily maintains; "we have to make conservation fit mainstream business calculations."[1] Thus, Daily meets with business leaders to explain the value of threatened ecosystems in terms of the services that these ecosystems provide to humankind. This, some believe, is the future of the conservation movement. According to journalist David Wolman, "Increasingly, economic measures are being used to assess ecosystems by way of the universally comprehensible currency of money."[2] Wolman cites, for example, the work of entomologists from Cornell University and the Xerces Society for Invertebrate Conservation. These researchers maintain that wild bugs contribute approximately $60 billion dollars a year to the U.S. economy. "Dung beetles and bees . . . pollinate plants, hasten the decomposition of manure, feed on crop pests and end up as dinner for birds, small mammals and fish." This type of national capital research has spurred conservationists worldwide to explore how best to define and measure nature's capital.

1. Quoted in David Wolman, "How to Get Wall Street to Hug a Tree," *Los Angeles Times*, February 11, 2007.
2. *Ibid.*

Resources for the Future scholar James Boyd asserts, "The benefits of nature are too important and too large to be 'left off the table' of national accounting."[3]

Some conservationists question whether calculating natural capital will help protect biodiversity. They challenge the idea that financial markets are adequate to protect threatened species. After Costa Rican coffee farmers learned that native bees provided $60,000 a year in pollination services, they agreed that protecting the nearby forests where the bees live was in their best interest. However, when coffee prices dropped, these farmers shifted to growing pineapples, which do not require pollination, thus taking away their motivation to preserve the forests. According to biologist Douglas J. McCauley, "If we oversell the message that ecosystems are important because they provide services, we will have effectively sold out nature."[4] These environmentalists argue that quantifying the economic benefits of biodiversity cannot replace conservation efforts for the sake of nature alone.

Partnering with business in any way raises serious red flags for some environmental activists. They find the concept of biodiversity offsets particularly dangerous. One of the major causes of biodiversity loss is the destruction of natural habitat by development—agriculture, mining, transportation, and construction, for example. Since nations rely on this development for economic growth, biodiversity often suffers. Some governments and nongovernmental organizations promote programs in which companies can offset the threats their activities pose by supporting other environmental concerns. "Now mining, oil and other corporations can not only enter a previous ecosystem and destroy it, but they can, through this destruction, create a brilliant business opportunity for biodiversity offsets," argues ecoactivist Simone Lovera. "That is, in cooperation with interested partners," she argues,

3. James Boyd, *The Nonmarket Benefits of Nature: What Should Be Counted in Green GDP?* Resources for the Future, May 2006.
4. Douglas J. McCauley, "Selling Out on Nature," *Nature*, September 7, 2006.

"they can set up a cute-looking protected area to 'compensate' for the destruction caused by their activities."[5] Companies who exploit offsets can often bitterly divide communities, detractors argue. "By throwing them a handful of jobs and a handful of beads . . . half of the community will become dependent on income from the offset,"[6] Lovera claims, creating friction with those who oppose the company's destructive environmental policies.

Some organizations such as the World Bank effectively impose conservation policies on developing nations by requiring these nations to conserve wildlife and habitat in order to receive development loans. Some leaders in developing nations resent this interference. They argue that it is unfair for wealthy, developed nations that long ago destroyed their own natural resources to ask developing nations to conserve habitat. Leaders in Brazil, for example, see rain forest conservation as an impediment to the economic benefits to be gained from building dams, highways, and ports. Lorenzo Carrasco, a Brazilian critic of Amazon conservation programs, asserts, "This is a new form of colonialism."[7]

Clearly, how best to promote biodiversity remains contentious. While some believe that people must be motivated to preserve nature for its own sake, others claim that creating economic motives is best. The authors in the following book, *At Issue: Biodiversity*, debate the importance of biodiversity, its potential threats, and how best to address these challenges. According to Thomas E. Lovejoy, Biodiversity Chair at the Heinz Center for Science, Economics and the Environment, an environmental think tank, these debates are critical. "That's the point of ranting and raving about it. It's not a matter of

5. Simone Lovera, "The Big Business of Biodiversity Destruction," *ECO*, December 1, 2005.
6. *Ibid.*
7. Quoted in Larry Rohter, "In the Amazon: Conservation or Colonialism?" *New York Times*, July 27, 2007.

whether we can prevent extinction entirely," he reasons; "the issue is whether we can still minimize it."[8]

8. Quoted in Tom Arrandale, "Disappearing Species," *CQ Researcher*, November 30, 2007.

The Biodiversity Controversy: An Overview

Tom Arrandale

Tom Arrandale, a freelance journalist from Montana who writes on environmental issues, is author of The Battle for Natural Resources.

Many biologists predict that more that 30,000 species are lost each year due to human activities such as overfishing, habitat destruction, and the release of the greenhouse gases that lead to global warming. While some believe the biodiversity loss is irreversible, others believe there still is hope if current efforts to conserve biodiversity are expanded. Still other commentators claim that these extinction numbers are exaggerated to promote costly solutions that may in fact be inadequate to reduce biodiversity declines. Also disputed is the impact of biodiversity loss on human welfare. Some claim, for example, that by ignoring declining biodiversity people risk losing potential life-saving medicines. Free-market scholars argue, on the other hand, that drug companies are no longer as interested in using wild plants and animals as medicine. The biodiversity debate remains contentious.

From tree frogs to African gorillas to Mediterranean sharks, some of Earth's most intriguing—and beloved—wild creatures face uncertain futures. Now biologists are predicting that two-thirds of the Northern Hemisphere's estimated 20,000 polar bears will disappear in the next 50 years. The cause: Warming temperatures are rapidly melting the Arctic ice, where they spend most of the year hunting seals and other mammals.

Tom Arrandale, "Disappearing Species," *CQ Researcher*, vol. 17, November 30, 2007, pp. 985–1008. Copyright © 2007 by CQ Press, a division of SAGE Publications, Inc. All rights reserved. Reproduced by permission.

"As the sea ice goes, so goes the polar bear," said Steven Amstrup, a biologist with the U.S. Geological Survey. The agency worries the bears could be extinct in three Arctic ecosystems within 75 years, with a smaller population barely hanging on along Canada's northern coast.

Hurtling Toward Oblivion

Throughout the world, thousands of other distinctive animals and plants may also be hurtling toward oblivion. India has only 1,500 tigers left, down 50 percent in the last six years, and poaching and habitat loss caused by growing human populations over the next 20 years could condemn tigers to "dwindle to the point of 'ecological extinction,' in which their numbers are too few to play their role as top predator in the ecosystem," said researchers for the World Wildlife Fund and other conservation organizations.

Even inside wildlife sanctuaries, illegal hunting for food and animal parts is taking a rising toll on tigers as well as Africa's gorillas, humans' closest primate relative. The International Union for Conservation of Nature and Natural Resources (IUCN), also known as the World Conservation Union, warns the combined toll from the Ebola virus and demand for "bush meat" has reduced the remnant population to critically endangered status, or put it on a downward spiral toward total annihilation in the wild.

The IUCN warned in an October [2007] report that nearly a third of the world's 394 known species of apes, monkeys, lemurs and other primates are now in danger of extinction. The study focused on 25 species imperiled by hunting, illegal wildlife trade and logging in the tropical forests that provide them with dwindling strongholds. In Ghana and Ivory Coast, a rare red colobus may already be gone, while remnants of Vietnam's golden-headed langur and China's Hainan gibbon number in the dozens.

"You could fit all the surviving members of these 25 species in a single football stadium; that's how few of them remain on Earth today," said Conservation International President Russell A. Mittermeier, who chairs the IUCN's primate panel.

Meanwhile, the IUCN recently added 188 more species to its "Red List" of threatened wildlife. In addition to the gorilla, new listings included the Sumatran orangutan, Indian crocodile, Asian red-headed vulture, two Galapagos Islands corals, Mexico's Santa Catalina Island rattlesnake and 10 seaweed species. A Malaysian herb, the woody-stalked Begonia, was listed as officially extinct, and China's Yangtze River dolphin was listed as possibly extinct.

The First Stages of Mass Extinction

But the most staggering species losses are likely among insects, amphibians and millions of even smaller organisms that inhabit remote tropical forests or deep ocean waters.

"Each species is a small piece of [the global threat], but it all adds up," says renowned tropical biologist Thomas E. Lovejoy, president of the Washington based Heinz Center for Science, Economics, and the Environment. Lovejoy, who coined the term "biological diversity" in 1980, concludes that "we're in the first stages of a mass extinction."

At current rates, "one-third to one-half of all species on Earth are predicted to be extinguished in the next century," adds Duke University conservation biologist Stuart Pimm. Biologists so far have described a total of 1.9 million species of plants and animals, but the IUCN has completed formal studies on the status of fewer than 3 percent. The total number of plants and animals on Earth, however, may be exponentially larger. E.O. Wilson, the famed Harvard University entomologist and best-selling author, reports that estimates of the actual number of species "range, according to the method used, from 3.6 million to 100 million or more."

The Pressures of Population

In the last 50 years, wildlife has come under increasing pressure as population exploded and Third World nations began developing tropical forests and other undeveloped lands to boost food production and stimulate lagging economies. In South America and Indonesia, settlers continue cutting and burning tropical forests that comprise the planet's most biologically rich ecosystems. Tropical rain forests cover only 6 percent of Earth's land surface, yet their terrestrial and aquatic habitats hold more than half of the world's known species. But the forests are being cut down at a devastating clip. Twenty percent of South America's Amazon rain forest has been lost in the last 40 years, and Africa's 800,000-square-mile Congo Basin rain forest also is rapidly being logged and converted to agricultural use.

We can clean up pollution, but we cannot re-create species. 'Jurassic Park' is a [movie] fantasy.

Twenty years ago, Duke University biologist Norman Myers identified 25 vulnerable areas, or "hot spots," that house 40 percent of the planet's species. Myers and other Conservation International scientists now have expanded the list to 34 regions, including 22 tropical forests. Most are in Africa, South America and Southeast Asia, but they also include parts of Australia, Japan, the Caucasus temperate forests, China, the Caribbean and the California Coast from Mexico to Oregon.

"We have cut much of the heart out of biodiversity," Wilson wrote. Many known insects, amphibians, microbes, fungi and rare plants are at severe risk, even as biologists continue to identify previously unknown species. Just in the last year, two new lizard species were found in Brazil. Also, scientific surveys in the Guinean forest of West Africa recorded three previously unknown bat species and found 16 more specimens of an endangered horseshoe bat that had been thought down to nine individuals.

As habitat destruction continues, however, biologists fear countless species are vanishing without ever being discovered and studied.

Big, visible animals with limited ranges and slow reproductive rates that live high on the food chain generally have been most vulnerable, such as carnivores and primates. Many mammals, birds, reptiles and fish are increasingly beset by polluted water, competition from exotic competitors and well-armed poachers and industrial fishing fleets. Now, climbing temperatures are an increasing factor. In addition to putting polar bears at risk by melting Arctic ice, global warming also is bleaching coral reefs and raising the acid content in seawater, killing off plankton and other crustaceans at the base of the marine food chain.

Disputing the Evidence

Some biologists and observers contend that evidence is too sketchy to conclude that a mass extinction has started. But others see evidence that cumulative human impacts are launching an ecological catastrophe that could prove more devastating than climate change by itself.

Others see some hope that humans will eventually recognize that preventing extinction of species is in their own best interest.

"To scientists, this is an unparalleled calamity, far more severe than global warming," University of Chicago biologist Jerry A. Coyne and Harvard University Professor Hopi E. Hoekstra recently warned. "Life as we know it would be impossible if ecosystems collapsed," they contend. "Yet that is where we're headed if species extinction continues at its current pace."

The Earth's accumulating loss of biodiversity "is huge and it's irreversible, and global warming isn't irreversible," adds

Duke University's Pimm. "Once you drive a species to extinction, it's gone." Pimm and Duke colleague Myers also describe biodiversity loss as "today's most significant environmental problem. We can clean up pollution, but we cannot re-create species. 'Jurassic Park' is a [movie] fantasy."

Yet, Pimm and others see some hope that humans will eventually recognize that preventing extinction of species is in their own best interest. Pimm and Myers note, for example, that "biodiversity conservation offers a host of spin-off benefits, like protecting watersheds that are essential for drinking water and fisheries." Besides, Pimm adds, "who would want to tell their kids that they witnessed the demise of lions and tigers and bears?"

As scientists study the viability of Earth's species and threatened habitats, here are key questions they are asking:

Is Mass Extinction Imminent?

Species have evolved and disappeared since life on Earth began nearly 4 billion years ago. Fossil records reveal at least five mass extinctions—the result of natural cataclysms—that eliminated most species, the most recent 65 million years ago. Over time, the world's biodiversity has always bounced back. But now some biologists fear human development of global resources is setting off a sixth mass extinction, one that could permanently impoverish global biological resources.

Up to 30,000 plant and animal species are now disappearing every year because of human activity, biologists estimate. The United Nations [U.N.] Environment Programme warned recently that "changes to biodiversity currently under way . . . are more rapid than at any time in human history." The IUCN calculates that species are now being lost at between 1,000 to as much as 10,000 times higher than the "background" rate at which natural evolutionary forces would cause them to vanish.

The IUCN's most recent "Red List" identifies more than 16,000 species as potentially threatened with extinction, including 12 percent of the birds, 20 percent of the mammals and 29 percent of the frogs, turtles and other amphibians that biologists have studied so far.

So far, roughly three-quarters of known extinctions have occurred on islands, where distinctive species that evolved separately from the rest of the world have been extremely vulnerable when humans began moving into their habitat, according to the U.N.'s *Millennium Ecosystem Assessment*. In the last two decades, however, biologists have found half of the extinctions on continental mainland, with tropical rain forests especially vulnerable.

Predicting future species losses 'is a very tricky thing, because everybody's overstating the case on every side of the debate.'

Biodiversity losses are compounded when native species are displaced by the competitors that thrive in the urban settings or farms that replace forests and other native ecosystems. A panel of *Millennium Assessment* biologists found that bird extinctions so far have been concentrated on oceanic islands, especially Hawaii and New Zealand. Sri Lanka has the highest number of recorded amphibian extinctions, but losses are accelerating in South American mountains and forests, Caribbean islands and Australia. Mammals are vanishing most rapidly in Australia and the Caribbean. Some species like the American bald eagle and peregrine falcon have rebounded, but scientists aren't optimistic that other declining plants and animals can be rescued as remaining wild habitat is chopped up. "Nature is resilient, but it's not resilient enough to overcome the changes we're now experiencing," the University of Chicago's Coyne says. "We're taking away all the space that it needs to come back."

The Skeptics

But skeptics contend that scientific data are too sketchy to conclude a biological holocaust is looming. Amy L. Kaleita, an expert on soil and water conservation at Iowa State University, agrees that "many ecosystems are quite delicate, and removing certain species or communities has consequences." However, "there are very few quantifiable measures of biodiversity," she adds. "Once you get to larger ecosystems, it becomes very difficult" to assess the extent of species losses.

Kaleita co-authored a 2007 assessment of environmental threats published by the conservative American Enterprise Institute and Pacific Research Institute arguing that whether or not global biodiversity "should be considered in 'crisis' depends on which guesstimate of the magnitude of the problem one finds most plausible. As usual, the more alarmist projections receive the most media notice."

In a recent *BioScience* article, several biologists concurred that "the information is so meager and poor that the evaluations in many cases are merely intelligent guesses." Predicting future species losses "is a very tricky thing, because everybody's overstating the case on every side of the debate," says co-author Daniel B. Botkin, a University of California-Santa Barbara biologist. Botkin himself works on saving whales and other endangered wildlife, but he worries that focusing debates on exaggerated warnings about mass extinctions based on questionable scientific assumptions are "moving people away from what they ought to be doing about saving species."

In his controversial 2001 book *The Skeptical Environmentalist,* Bjorn Lomborg, a Danish professor of statistics, contended that a commonly used forecast of losing 40,000 species every year "has become part of our environmental litany." Yet that commonly accepted figure is based on assumptions that if 90 percent of a habitat is removed, half the species found there will vanish, he says. But Lomborg notes that the species/ area relationship has not held up: When biologists attempted to count species numbers in the transformed habitats of Eastern North America, Brazil's Atlantic Coast forests and Puerto Rico, the rate of extinction turned out to be much less dramatic, he says. Lomborg notes that more cautious models agree that extinctions are climbing above natural levels—but at a rate of only about 0.7 percent every 50 years, much smaller than the most alarming projections. Losing that many "over a limited time span is not a catastrophe but a problem—one of many that mankind still needs to solve," he contends.

In fact, Seymour Garte, a professor of environmental and occupational health at the University of Pittsburgh, says worst-case predictions of mass extinctions overlook real progress in preserving habitat and restoring endangered species in North America and other developed areas. But Garte concurs that habitat destruction is taking a heavy toll on biodiversity in the Amazon and Southeast Asian rain forests. "They've got it half right," Garte says. "We really don't know what's going on." . . .

Will Losing Species Impair Human Well-Being?

Many experts say humans will pay a price if too many species are lost. As species disappear, the ecosystems they live in are also collapsing or disappearing, taking with them sources of pure water, food and other necessities. "Human activities have taken the planet to the edge of a massive wave of species extinctions, further threatening our own well-being," the 2005 *Millennium Ecosystem Assessment* declared.

Experts disagree, however, over whether keeping entire ecosystems intact will be as essential for human communities as it is for wild plants and animals. In a widely reported estimate a decade ago, economists and environmental scientists calculated that ecosystems contribute $33 trillion or more a year in materials, energy and other services that benefit human communities.

Disappearing honeybees demonstrate the potential for calamity if key species vanish. American bee colony numbers have fallen 40 percent in the last 60 years, and last winter about a quarter of American beekeepers began reporting heavy losses of bees that failed to return to hives. Some blamed the puzzling phenomenon, dubbed "colony collapse disorder," on global warming. Preliminary findings, however, pointed to a paralyzing virus, possibly carried by bees imported from Australia.

Nonetheless, the honeybee losses demonstrated how the sophisticated agricultural industry still relies on wild pollinators. In many other ways, the World Resources Institute declared in a 2005 *Millennium Ecosystem Assessment* that "biodiversity and human well-being are inextricably linked." The Earth's natural ecological bounty supplies clean air, water, food and other "ecosystem services" human communities need to survive. Coastal mangroves and wetlands protect humans by absorbing the fury of tropical storms and hurricanes, for instance. Forests and grasslands store water, retard floods, and purify the air—keeping even the most urbanized cities livable.

Declining biodiversity . . . may encourage the spread to humans of serious wildlife-born diseases.

Improving Human Life, Weakening Nature

In the *Millennium Assessment*, more than 1,300 experts concluded that meeting human requirements for food, water, fiber and energy is putting unprecedented pressure on productive ecosystems. While the resulting changes have helped to improve the lives of billions, they wrote, "at the same time they weakened nature's ability to deliver other key services such as purification of air and water, protection from disasters, and the provision of medicines. . . . [T]he ability of the planet's ecosystems to sustain future generations can no longer be taken for granted."

In a notable example, commercial fishing catches peaked in the 1980s, but at least a quarter of valuable marine fish are still being harvested at rates that can't be sustained. Overfishing caused the Newfoundland cod fishery to collapse in 1992, costing 20,000 jobs. In the Pacific Northwest, an estimated 72,000 jobs have vanished because salmon runs have been depleted by dams and habitat losses.

Declining biodiversity also may encourage the spread to humans of serious wildlife-born diseases like Lyme disease, avian influenza and West Nile virus. For generations, native societies have converted wild plants and animals into medicines and herbal remedies. A 2002 Harvard Medical School report found that commonly used drugs for humans were being made from 119 chemical compounds derived from 90 plant species. The bark of the Pacific yew tree, for instance, yields taxol, a drug effective in treating breast and ovarian cancer. The Madagascar periwinkle's sap produces another anti-cancer drug, while tree bark is used to make aspirin and quinine. Scientists says that only a small portion of plants and animals have been screened for potential life-saving pharmaceuticals, and "the search for natural medicinals is a race between science and extinction," entomologist Wilson warns.

"If we value the life sciences, we shouldn't wreck the fundamental library on which they're built," says the Heinz Center's Lovejoy. "We're losing the books without even reading them."

Free-enterprise advocates acknowledge that some visible species are in trouble, but they caution against overreacting to dire predictions. Sally Satel, a physician and American Enterprise Institute scholar, says wild plants and animals are growing less important to drug researchers, who she says are now focusing on screening synthetic molecules for leads on new medications. Satel calls "bioprospecting" for useful wild plants and animals a "high risk and very low yield venture" that amounts to "a small and shrinking percentage of the portfolio of major drug companies."

Even some biologists say that human benefits from protecting species are difficult to demonstrate. "In truth, ecologists and conservationists have struggled to demonstrate the increased material benefits to humans of 'intact' wild systems" over lands now being used for farming and other purposes, contends Martin Jenkins, a U.N. Environment Programme biologist. "In terms of the most direct benefits, the reverse is indeed obviously the case; this is the logic that has driven us to convert some 1.5 billion hectares of land area to highly productive, managed and generally low-diversity systems under agriculture."

Even considering general ecological services, Jenkins says developed landscapes managed and maintained by humans can provide what communities require. "Where increased benefits of natural systems have been shown, they are usually marginal and local," he adds.

2

Biodiversity Helps Humans Appreciate the Gifts of Life

Frank Carpenter

Frank Carpenter, retired pastor of St. Johns Unitarian Universalist Church in Cincinnati, Ohio, is a graduate of the Massachusetts Institute of Technology, where he studied biology and the history of science.

People can learn to better understand their own nature by learning from their shared nature with animals and the biodiversity of life on Earth. Some fear seeing themselves as animals because animals can be violent. However, animals also can be compassionate and empathetic. Understanding the benefits of biodiversity also can teach people about the importance of cultural diversity. People can learn valuable lessons from different cultures. For example, the Amish in Nickel Mines, Pennsylvania, chose to forgive and avoid hostility, even in the face of the murder of their children. Biodiversity therefore should be cherished as it offers hope for humanity.

Six years ago [2002] when Jacquie and I were meeting with you [the congregation of St. John's Unitarian Universalist Church in Cincinnati, Ohio] to explore if I would become your minister, among Jacquie's prime interests was the zoo. The first chance she got, she walked there. She is a walker, but I was still struck that she could walk from the Zoo to St. John's. Since then we have taken out a Family Membership. If we had our druthers, [we] would visit the zoo several times a

Frank Carpenter, "Sermon: Biodiversity Sunday," St. John's Unitarian Universalist Church, August 17, 2008. Reproduced by permission of the author.

week. Our first interest was the red pandas, then the gibbons, then the Siberian lynx. Most recently, I have been taken with the shrine to the last passenger pigeon Martha, and the last Carolina parakeet, Incas. The Siberian lynx spends his days gazing out on the statue of Martha which is at the entrance to the pagoda which relates the story of Incas and Martha. . . .

Passing through Kentucky in 1813 John James Audubon, the eminent naturalist and bird artist spoke of a mass migration of passenger pigeons: "the air was literally filled with pigeons; the light of noonday was obscured as by an eclipse." For three days the pigeons poured out of the Northeast in search of forests bearing nuts and acorns. By Audubon's estimate, the flock that passed overhead contained more than 1 billion birds, a number consistent with calculations by other ornithologists [bird studiers]. As the pigeons approached their roost, Audubon noted that the noise they made "reminded me of a hard gale at sea passing through the rigging of a close-reefed vessel."

Biodiversity, respect for the [interdependent] web, is not only a matter of aesthetics, of earth based spirituality; it's also a matter of humbly recognizing our true place in the order of things.

Passenger pigeons lived in a part of America where humans also wanted to live. Farm crops became a substitute food supply, making passenger pigeons a locust-like threat to farmers. Since passenger pigeons only lived in huge flocks, they were easy to kill in staggering numbers. In 1878, a flock of passenger pigeons in Michigan were shot and clubbed to death at a rate of 50,000 birds a day, every day, for nearly five months.

The last pigeon to go was "Martha"—named for Martha Washington—who fell off of her perch and died in 1914 at the advanced age of 29 in the Cincinnati Zoo.

An Interdependent Web

I am struck by how we have here in Cincinnati this symbol of what we as humans are doing to the ecology which gave birth to us on our planet. Passenger pigeons were not just some isolated creature that could be gotten rid of. Passenger pigeons, just as are dogs and cats, spiders, snakes and human beings, are all part of the interdependent web of all existence, as we say in the 7th principle.[1] The passenger pigeon played an important role in the ecological web. With the pigeons gone in the early 1900's, their primary food, acorns, began to flourish. Shortly thereafter, the population of deer and mice, which also subsist on acorns, began to explode as did the ticks these animals carry. Scientists now directly link the disappearance of the passenger pigeon to the spread of Lyme disease. Biodiversity, respect for the [interdependent] web, is not only a matter of aesthetics, of earth based spirituality; it's also a matter of humbly recognizing our true place in the order of things.

There were consequences of removing passenger pigeons from the interdependent web. Often, people think they can neglect that human beings are part of the web. An aspect of respecting the diversity of plants and animals is also seeing within that diversity a sameness. With all species, plants and animals, we are made up of cells that have DNA molecules controlling chemical pathways. . . . Most of us can identify with the bonobo who holds her child, the lazy gorilla napping, and the snarling lynx defending her territory.

Humans Behaving Badly

When we start comparing ourselves to animals, saying that humans are animals, there are connotations of human beings as savages, barbarians. We all know, 'animals are violent.' Right? If animals are violent. does that mean human beings are inherently violent? Perhaps one of the reasons people avoid thinking of humans as animals is to avoid coming to terms with inherent violent impulses.

1. Unitarian Universalist Congregations affirm seven guiding principles.

But we know human beings are violent. Just go south a few miles to Big Bone Lick, KY, State Park. There you can read the story of the extinction of the great mammals in North America: mammoths and mastodons disappeared with the coming of the first human beings on the North American continent. This is August, the time we recall the [1945] bombings of Hiroshima and Nagasaki [Japan]. In the early 1920's, my Father lived for a year and a half in Nagasaki, so each August 9th I think of him, and the home he lived in, now gone. . . .

The Lessons of Biodiversity

And here again I think biodiversity gives us some hope. If biodiversity helps us understand violence, it also helps us comprehend empathy. Empathy is hard wired to some extent. We see it wandering about the zoo, watching animals care for young. The Cincinnati zoo does a lot to address endangered species. We see empathy across species at the Nursery near the Children's Zoo. You can watch Mashka, a mother cat, nurture infant mammals.

More than that, the zoo is a great revelation when it comes to human diversity. I think our Zoo is a great place for people watching. One of my favorite moments was at the elephant show when the keeper was talking about giving the elephants their Hollywood bath. In attendance were a number of youth wearing tee shirts identifying them as deaf. It was fascinating watching the signer with a very straight face sign the accounting of the keeper, as first he welcomed the deaf students, then talked about the elephants squirting and peeing into the pond. What made it doubly fascinating was the interest in the deaf of a young Amish woman. She had on a checkered dress and white cap, and was taking pictures of the deaf signer with a digital camera. It was an amazing snapshot of different kinds of diversity: biological and cultural.

Never have I seen so many Amish families as at the Zoo. It is fascinating for me to see the different families. They seem to each have the different colored shirts that identify them as belonging to one clan or another. Some speak English, others German. I was delighted one day to see a young Amish family walking up towards the former giraffe house. The mother had on the white cap the women wear and he the straw hat, and their usual dress. In front of them were a young boy and girl, about seven or eight, identically dressed as their parents, with the young girl pushing a baby carriage.

Our Shared Nature

Whenever I see the Amish, I remember the gift of grace and forgiveness which they gave our nation. On October 2, 2006, in an Amish schoolhouse in Nickel Mines, Pennsylvania five girls were shot dead and five wounded. On the anniversary a year later, the Nickel Mines community released a statement:

> "The Amish do not wish publicity for doing what Jesus taught and want to make sure that glory is given to God for that witness ... forgiveness is a journey ... you need help from your community and from God ... to make and hold on to a decision to not become a hostage to hostility. It is understood that hostility destroys community. The strength of community in Nickel Mines helps the families cope with this event that changed their lives forever. Sharing their experiences with family and friends in the church community through frequent visiting and repeated conversation, along with constantly available help in their work and other needs, are essential components of the healing process."

If we keep in mind our shared humanity with these good people. If we keep in mind our shared humanity with those not as good. If we keep in mind our shared biological nature with all creatures, great and small, on this planet, the gifts of grace and forgiveness, hope and peace, can be ours as well.

In the words of Charles Darwin,

If we choose to let conjecture run wild, then animals, our fellow brethren in pain, disease, suffering, and famine—our slaves in the most laborious works, our companions in our amusements—they may partake of our origins in one common ancestor—we may be all melted together.

The gift of biodiversity is life, is hope. Let us cherish this great gift and pass it on to each and all.

3

Biodiversity Is Important to Human Welfare

International Union for Conservation of Nature

Comprising governments, non-governmental organizations, and scientists worldwide, the International Union for Conservation of Nature (IUCN) promotes pragmatic solutions to environmental problems, particularly in the developing world.

Biodiversity is necessary for physical, cultural, and spiritual survival. Humans depend on biodiversity not only for food and shelter but also for relaxation and inspiration. Unfortunately, many people have become so far removed from nature that unsustainable development and consumerism continue unabated, posing a serous threat to the biodiversity necessary to human welfare. Media-driven doomsday attitudes add to the problem by making it more difficult to deliver the message that efforts to reduce biodiversity loss are necessary.

Take your pick: A world in which we all dress the same, speak the same language, eat the same food and listen to the same music. All our natural areas are ploughed up for roads, buildings and corn plantations, and all that's left of wildlife are battery-farmed chickens and dairy cows—a world without diversity.

Or, a world that is prosperous, peaceful, healthy, colourful, vibrant and resilient—in short, a diverse and sustainable world.

The Key to Resilience

There is growing recognition that diversity—biological as well as linguistic and cultural diversity—is the lifeblood of sustainable development and human welfare. Diversity is key to resilience—the ability of natural and social systems to adapt to change. Every week brings news of yet another devastating flood, landslide or hurricane while the conservation community shakes its head in dismay—protecting people from the full force of these disasters could be so simple and so cheap if we let nature act as a buffer.

Mankind has drawn on diversity throughout history, for basic needs such as food and shelter, but also in much deeper cultural and spiritual ways. People are drawn to the beauty of nature for recreation, relaxation and inspiration. In recent years, we're seeing diversity in increasingly practical terms—as a source of cures to diseases and helping us adapt to changing conditions such as global warming.

But we are rapidly losing diversity, despite all the warnings. We know that ancient civilizations collapsed because of environmental damage. We understand how monocultures contributed to agricultural disasters like the Irish Potato Famine.[1] Excessive development and consumerism are destroying our natural systems, standardizing landscapes and eroding cultures. Stress, obesity and community breakdown are increasing rapidly. We know current growth rates are not sustainable and are not leading to the life we want. The world knows it has to change and has the means to do so. So what's stopping us?

In the western world, we have become so far removed from biodiversity that we've forgotten how much we use it in our daily lives and how seriously we're affected by its loss. When we eat a wild salmon steak, we rarely think of the spe-

---

1. The Irish potato famine was a period of mass starvation and disease in Ireland between 1845 and 1852, during which approximately 1 million people died and a million more emigrated to other nations.

cies that the salmon depends on to thrive. When we fell a mature tree to make a table, we lose a host of lichens and invertebrates; part of an entire web of life is lost. Yet people in the developing world know exactly what's at stake as they set out each morning to gather fuelwood from a dwindling forest, travel ever farther to hunt animals for food and collect medicinal plants to treat their sick children.

In the western world, we have become so far removed from biodiversity that we've forgotten how much we use it in our daily lives and how seriously we're affected by its loss.

Keeping the Battle Alive

While many believe we're on a fast-track to self-destruction, many others refute this apocalyptic world vision. They believe the battle is alive in keeping the world's myriad landscapes, species, cultures and languages intact. They say the mainstream media is largely to blame for peddling feelings of doom and gloom and, that with awareness of environmental and social issues at an all-time high, the tide is finally turning. The world is connecting as never before. As Paul Hawken puts it in *Blessed Unrest*, the combined environmental and social movements have, like nature itself, organized from the bottom up, in every city, town and culture, from multimillion dollar NGOs [non-governmental organizations] to single-person causes, and are expressing people's needs worldwide. We are starting to reconnect with our environment and with each other.

But this issue [of *World Conservation* magazine] isn't dedicated to *how* we save diversity, it's about *why* we need it in the first place. Conservationists feel they are banging their heads against a wall because the rest of the world doesn't seem to be listening. Or, more likely, we're not doing very well at getting the message across. That's why . . . we're going back to basics, asking the question: How can we expect to tackle poverty and climate change if we don't look after the natural wealth of animals, plants, microorganisms and ecosystems that make our planet inhabitable? By making the scientific, social, economic and cultural case for keeping diversity, [conservationists] highlight just how much [diversity] supports nearly every aspect of human life. But the arguments for conserving biological and cultural diversity should not be all utilitarian. For many people, we should save it simply because it exists, and has done for millennia.

If we don't hurry up and convince governments, politicians, business leaders and the public why we need diversity and how urgent it is that they mobilize to save it, the world will move on and our fate will be sealed. We need to do better at showing how much progress has been made and how much more can be done. It's time to get our collective act together. . . .

4

Mass Species Extinction Poses a Serious Threat

Jerry Coyne and Hopi E. Hoekstra

Jerry Coyne is a professor in the Department of Ecology and Evolution at the University of Chicago. Hopi E. Hoekstra is associate professor in the Department of Organismic and Evolutionary Biology at Harvard University and curator of mammals at Harvard's Museum of Comparative Zoology.

Earth is experiencing a mass extinction due to human activities that pose a serious threat to biodiversity. Tropical rainforests are vanishing, fisheries are failing, and great apes have nearly disappeared from the wild. Unfortunately for humanity, the consequences of this mass extinction are dire. The destruction of rainforests aggravates the problem of global warming and increases the spread of disease. Overfishing and pollution threaten the aquatic food web on which many in the world depend. For some biologists, the destruction of thousands of species for monetary gain is also a moral failure, as they know that humans share a common genetic heritage with all creatures. Indeed, exploiting Earth's biodiversity may lead to the extinction of humankind.

Two hundred fifty million years ago, a monumental catastrophe devastated life on Earth. We don't know the cause—perhaps glaciers, volcanoes, or even the impact of a giant meteorite—but whatever happened drove more than 90 percent of the planet's species to extinction. After the Great

Dying, as the end-Permian extinction is called, Earth's biodiversity—its panoply of species—didn't bounce back for more than ten million years.

A Human-Caused Mass Extinction

Aside from the Great Dying, there have been four other mass extinctions, all of which severely pruned life's diversity. Scientists agree that we're now in the midst of a sixth such episode. This new one, however, is different—and, in many ways, much worse. For, unlike earlier extinctions, this one results from the work of a single species, Homo sapiens. We are relentlessly taking over the planet, laying it to waste and eliminating most of our fellow species.

Moreover, we're doing it much faster than the mass extinctions that came before. Every year, up to 30,000 species disappear due to human activity alone. At this rate, we could lose half of Earth's species in this century. And, unlike with previous extinctions, there's no hope that biodiversity will ever recover, since the cause of the decimation—us—is here to stay.

To scientists, this is an unparalleled calamity, far more severe than global warming, which is, after all, only one of many threats to biodiversity. Yet global warming gets far more press. Why? One reason is that, while the increase in temperature is easy to document, the decrease of species is not. Biologists don't know, for example, exactly how many species exist on Earth. Estimates range widely, from three million to more than 50 million, and that doesn't count microbes, critical (albeit invisible) components of ecosystems. We're not certain about the rate of extinction, either; how could we be, since the vast majority of species have yet to be described? We're even less sure how the loss of some species will affect the ecosystems in which they're embedded, since the intricate connection between organisms means that the loss of a single species can ramify unpredictably.

But we do know some things. Tropical rainforests are disappearing at a rate of 2 percent per year. Populations of most large fish are down to only 10 percent of what they were in 1950. Many primates and all the great apes—our closest relatives—are nearly gone from the wild.

As extinction increases, then, so does global warming, which in turn causes more extinction—and so on, into a downward spiral of destruction.

A Destructive Synergy

And we know that extinction and global warming act synergistically. Extinction exacerbates global warming: By burning rainforests, we're not only polluting the atmosphere with carbon dioxide (a major greenhouse gas) but destroying the very plants that can remove this gas from the air. Conversely, global warming increases extinction, both directly (killing corals) and indirectly (destroying the habitats of Arctic and Antarctic animals). As extinction increases, then, so does global warming, which in turn causes more extinction—and so on, into a downward spiral of destruction.

Why, exactly, should we care? Let's start with the most celebrated case: the rainforests. Their loss will worsen global warming—raising temperatures, melting icecaps, and flooding coastal cities. And, as the forest habitat shrinks, so begins the inevitable contact between organisms that have not evolved together, a scenario played out many times, and one that is never good. Dreadful diseases have successfully jumped species boundaries, with humans as prime recipients. We have gotten AIDS from apes, SARS from civets, and Ebola from fruit bats. Additional worldwide plagues from unknown microbes are a very real possibility.

But it isn't just the destruction of the rainforests that should trouble us. Healthy ecosystems the world over provide hidden services like waste disposal, nutrient cycling, soil formation, water purification, and oxygen production. Such services are best rendered by ecosystems that are diverse. Yet, through both intention and accident, humans have introduced exotic species that turn biodiversity into monoculture. Fast-growing zebra mussels, for example, have outcompeted more than 15 species of native mussels in North America's Great Lakes and have damaged harbors and water-treatment plants. Native prairies are becoming dominated by single species (often genetically homogenous) of corn or wheat. Thanks to these developments, soils will erode and become unproductive—which, along with temperature change, will diminish agricultural yields. Meanwhile, with increased pollution and runoff, as well as reduced forest cover, ecosystems will no longer be able to purify water; and a shortage of clean water spells disaster.

In many ways, oceans are the most vulnerable areas of all. As overfishing eliminates major predators, while polluted and warming waters kill off phytoplankton, the intricate aquatic food web could collapse from both sides. Fish, on which so many humans depend, will be a fond memory. As phytoplankton vanish, so does the ability of the oceans to absorb carbon dioxide and produce oxygen. (Half of the oxygen we breathe is made by phytoplankton, with the rest coming from land plants.) Species extinction is also imperiling coral reefs—a major problem since these reefs have far more than recreational value: They provide tremendous amounts of food for human populations and buffer coastlines against erosion.

In fact, the global value of "hidden" services provided by ecosystems—those services, like waste disposal, that aren't bought and sold in the marketplace—has been estimated to be as much as $50 trillion per year, roughly equal to the gross domestic product of all countries combined. And that doesn't include tangible goods like fish and timber. Life as we know it would be impossible if ecosystems collapsed. Yet that is where we're heading if species extinction continues at its current pace.

The Impact on Medicine

Extinction also has a huge impact on medicine. Who really cares if, say, a worm in the remote swamps of French Guiana goes extinct? Well, those who suffer from cardiovascular disease. The recent discovery of a rare South American leech has led to the isolation of a powerful enzyme that, unlike other anticoagulants, not only prevents blood from clotting but also dissolves existing clots. And it's not just this one species of worm: Its wriggly relatives have evolved other biomedically valuable proteins, including antistatin (a potential anticancer agent), decorsin and ornatin (platelet aggregation inhibitors), and hirudin (another anticoagulant).

It is certain that our future is bleak if we do nothing to stem this sixth extinction.

Plants, too, are pharmaceutical gold mines. The bark of trees, for example, has given us quinine (the first cure for malaria), taxol (a drug highly effective against ovarian and breast cancer), and aspirin. More than a quarter of the medicines on our pharmacy shelves were originally derived from plants. The sap of the Madagascar periwinkle contains more than 70 useful alkaloids, including vincristine, a powerful anticancer drug that saved the life of one of our friends.

Of the roughly 250,000 plant species on Earth, fewer than 5 percent have been screened for pharmaceutical properties. Who knows what life-saving drugs remain to be discovered? Given current extinction rates, it's estimated that we're losing one valuable drug every two years.

The Spiritual Value of Genetic Kinship

Our arguments so far have tacitly assumed that species are worth saving only in proportion to their economic value and their effects on our quality of life, an attitude that is strongly ingrained, especially in Americans. That is why conservationists always base their case on an economic calculus. But we biologists know in our hearts that there are deeper and equally compelling reasons to worry about the loss of biodiversity: namely, simple morality and intellectual values that transcend pecuniary interests. What, for example, gives us the right to destroy other creatures? And what could be more thrilling than looking around us, seeing that we are surrounded by our evolutionary cousins, and realizing that we all got here by the same simple process of natural selection? To biologists, and potentially everyone else, apprehending the genetic kinship and common origin of all species is a spiritual experience— not necessarily religious, but spiritual nonetheless, for it stirs the soul.

But, whether or not one is moved by such concerns, it is certain that our future is bleak if we do nothing to stem this sixth extinction. We are creating a world in which exotic diseases flourish but natural medicinal cures are lost; a world in which carbon waste accumulates while food sources dwindle; a world of sweltering heat, failing crops, and impure water. In the end, we must accept the possibility that we ourselves are not immune to extinction. Or, if we survive, perhaps only a few of us will remain, scratching out a grubby existence on a devastated planet. Global warming will seem like a secondary problem when humanity finally faces the consequences of what we have done to nature: not just another Great Dying, but perhaps the greatest dying of them all.

5

Mass Species Extinction Is Exaggerated

Peter Foster

Peter Foster, who obtained a degree in economics from Cambridge University, is a Canadian journalist and author who emigrated from England in 1976, after having written for London's Financial Times. *He has written on economics issues for several Canadian publications and now writes editorials for the* Financial Post.

The facts do not support claims that the Earth is experiencing a mass extinction. Many organizations, agencies, and laws work to protect plants and wildlife, and the human impact on other species is real. Unfortunately, however, policy makers whose goal it is to promote their environmental agenda exploit extinction statistics by exaggerating the losses. Some conservation scientists and organizations base their mass extinction figures on the assumption that actual extinction rates can be applied to millions of yet undiscovered species. Actual observations, however, do not back up the claims. Mass extinction is, in fact, a myth.

Last month [August 2007] I was with my daughter at the famous Field Museum of Natural History in Chicago when I came across an arresting exhibit. Its message: Humans are destroying life on earth at an apocalyptic rate.

An Apocalyptic Message

According to the display, which was for some reason illustrated by a dead swan (a species which as far as I know is in no danger of extinction): "[F]or the first time in Earth's history, a single species is the primary cause of a mass extinction. Early on, extreme climate and environment change may have led to species loss. But today, human activity is destroying habitats, causing species to go extinct at a rapid rate. What has died? Almost too much to count. Scientists estimate we've lost 30,000 species in the last year. But because the earth is home to far more species than we've identified, there are surely many species going extinct unnoticed."

To bring home this terrifying message, there was a clock indicating the "Number for species that have gone extinct since 8:00 this morning." The culprits were identified as garbage, population, transportation, industry and logging. In other words, humanity. We should, presumably, feel both ashamed and horrified.

This grim picture seemed to be confirmed by the release yesterday [September 12, 2007] of the World Conservation Union's (IUCN) annual "Red List of Threatened Species." "Extinction crisis escalates," declared the press release. "Red List shows apes, corals, cultures, dolphins all in danger." It then proceeded to claim that "Life on Earth is disappearing fast and will continue to do so unless urgent action is taken."

According to Julia Marton-Lefevre, director-general of the IUCN, the "invaluable" efforts made so far "are not enough. We need to act now to stave off this global extinction crisis. This can be done, but only with a concerted effort by all levels of society." Presumably those levels would stretch from frightened schoolchildren through anti-development NGOs [nongovernmental organizations], huge self-serving international bureaucracies such as the IUCN, and national government environmental agencies, to, of course, the United Nations. As it says at the bottom of that press release: "To help IUCN in its fight against the extinction crisis, donate now."

Exploiting Extinction

How could I be so cynical? Well, step this way and I'll show you.

There can be no denying that the astonishing proliferation of the human race, and its stunning technology, have had an impact on other life forms. It could hardly be otherwise. What makes us unique, however, is that we care. Even capitalists.

There is always one clear sign of those seeking to exploit any 'problem' for political purposes: They will grossly exaggerate it.

Although there are many symbiotic relationships in nature, humans are unique in seeking to preserve fauna and flora. Apart from, but related to, intelligence, two of the characteristics that make humans different from other animals are sympathy—the fact that we can put ourselves in the position of others and "feel" both with and for them—and anthropomorphic projection, the fact that we attribute human characteristics to animals and even inanimate objects. The second may be a cognitive "error," but it fuels concern, and makes for wonderful flights of imagination. A purely "rational" species of intelligent beings would look with incomprehension at the work of A.A. Milne, Beatrix Potter or Walt Disney. Human concern for nature is also seen in the rapid growth of well-funded environmental organizations in recent decades, and in the enormous array of policy instruments—from national parks and wildlife reserves to endangered species and other laws—to protect plants, wildlife, and "the environment."

But there are less attractive aspects of human nature, and one of them is the tendency to exploit humanity's finer instincts in pursuit of power, pelf [monetary gain] and status.

Hence "biodiversity" has been turned into a political issue, which has been taken up by the United Nations—that fount of repressed and/or reflexive socialism—and used as an excuse for bureaucratic empire building, cheered on by many well-meaning, and sometimes well-funded, professional naturalists.

Amping the Facts

There is always one clear sign of those seeking to exploit any "problem" for political purposes: They will grossly exaggerate it. This is frequently seen as morally justifiable. After all, action needs to be taken. So what's wrong with amping the facts?

Plenty.

Biodiversity is firmly and deliberately linked to alleged man-made climate change. It is the twin, and related, alleged "crisis" seized upon by the radical environmental movement and its power- and place-seeking promoters to justify radically curtailing economic activity. As such, an alleged ongoing "biotic holocaust" has become a central, unquestionable, tenet of radical environmentalism. But is it true?

To lose one and a half species a year is a cause for sorrow; to claim there are another 29,998.5 that went extinct without us knowing their names is, well, suspicious.

For a start, let's take a look at one glaring "fact:" the enormous discrepancy in the extinction numbers between the Field Museum and the IUCN. According to the IUCN, and despite its apocalyptic language, the total number of species that has gone extinct (since 1500) "has reached 785 and a further 65 are only found in captivity or cultivation." That's about 1.5 species a year. How can that figure possibly fit with the Field Museum's claims that the earth is losing 30,000 a year, and what does that tell us about the biodiversity "crisis"? . . .

Declaring a species extinct is a ticklish business. How do you establish that something has disappeared off the face of the earth? Just this week, it was announced that tigers have been discovered in an Indian rainforest from which they were thought to have been wiped out three decades ago. Figures on species loss, however, are more than a thorny scientific matter. They are intensely political. . . .

Suspicious Figures

There are now 41,415 species on the "Red List" of the World Conservation Union (IUCN), 16,306 of which are allegedly "threatened with extinction." But "threatened" is not extinct. Indeed, to appear on the Red List virtually guarantees a frenzy of costly restorative action, which is, by and large, a good thing (as long as humans aren't sacrificed in the process).

However, when it comes to actual recorded extinctions, the IUCN acknowledges 785 over the past 500 years. That is, around 1 1/2 a year. The Field Museum claims species are going extinct at the rate of 30,000 annually. That's quite a difference. [Playwright] Oscar Wilde's Lady Bracknell famously declared that: "To lose one parent, Mr. Worthing, may be regarded as a misfortune; to lose both looks like carelessness." We might similarly reflect that to lose one and a half species a year is a cause for sorrow; to claim there are another 29,998.5 that went extinct without us knowing their names is, well, suspicious.

I contacted the Field's PR [public relations] department and was originally told that the 30,000 figure was taken from the work of Edward O. Wilson, a "world-renowned scientist." True. But E.O. Wilson isn't just any old Pulitzer Prize-winning Harvard boffin. He has an intriguing background in scientific controversy.

Scientific Controversy

In the 1970s, Prof. Wilson was at the centre of an academic slugfest over the implications of Darwinism for human nature and human society. In his book *Sociobiology*, Prof. Wilson claimed that to understand society, we had to understand man's evolved biological nature. For this quite obvious suggestion he was pilloried by Marxist academics as a determinist, genocidal racist, and promoter of the capitalist "status quo." These slurs were particularly painful to the professor, since he considered himself, like most academics, particularly at Harvard, "of the left."

According to the brilliant book *Defenders of the Truth*, by Ullica Segerstralle, the attacks on Prof. Wilson led to a remarkable personal transformation. By the end of the 1980s, Prof. Wilson had "reinvented" himself, she wrote, "from Wilson I, the politically incorrect sociobiologist, to Wilson II, the politically correct environmentalist. Here Wilson—supported by a general neo-catastrophist trend with tales of dinosaur deaths, asteroids, and the like—was able to make a convincing case for the importance of the preservation of biodiversity."

Since the alleged catastrophic loss of biodiversity was yet another alleged adverse side-effect of "untrammelled" capitalism, Prof. Wilson was now once more on-side with his old buddies on the left. Significantly, he is a member of the board of the David Suzuki Foundation. According to the Suzuki Web site, Professor Wilson believes that "The David Suzuki Foundation embodies the principles of scientific environmentalism."

Does that ring any alarm bells about objectivity?

Questionable Calculations

In fact, the huge extinction figures come from pure assumptions, which are based on the alleged implications of "habitat loss." These assumptions relate to the "background" rate of extinction, the number of undiscovered species on earth, and how much present rates of extinction might be above background rates due to human activity. They are, in other words, axe-grinding speculation. Cubed.

The calculations work like this: You assume that the "background" rate of extinction is, say, one species per million species per year. Then you estimate that there are 30 million species on earth (versus the 1.9 million so far classified). Then you assume that the present rate of extinction is, what the hell, say a thousand times the background level. Hence you arrive at a figure of 30,000 by assuming vast numbers of species that have never been identified and may not exist, the vast majority of which are, moreover, not pandas but notional bugs and bacteria.

Actual observations of habitat loss in no way backed up apocalyptic extinction estimates.

This means that the most egregious error at the Field Museum exhibit is the claim that "because the Earth is home to far more species than we've identified, there are surely many species going extinct unnoticed." But all the claimed 30,000 extinctions are "unnoticed." The Field cannot name any of them.

This is not considered a problem by the most radical proponents of global action to prevent the ravages of capitalism. Gro Harlem Brundtland, whose 1987 UN [United Nations] report is in many ways at the root of socialism's highly successful environmental counterthrust, has put it this way: "The library of life is burning, and we don't even know the titles of the books."

Prof. Wilson's figures have come under attack, but only by the brave. Dr. Patrick Moore, the now apostate founding member of Greenpeace, suggested that the only place you could find the alleged plethora of lost species was in Prof. Wilson's computer: "They're actually electrons on a hard drive."

Similarly, Bjorn Lomborg, in his much reviled but little refuted book, *The Skeptical Environmentalist*, noted that actual observations of habitat loss in no way backed up apocalyptic extinction estimates. For example, he pointed out that the forest of the Eastern United States had been reduced to fragments totalling just 1% to 2% of its previous area. This had resulted in the recorded extinction of one forest bird!

'Hard' figures, despite the hysterical spin put on them, suggest that the 'biotic holocaust' is a myth.

You might imagine that the slight matter of a factor difference of 20,000 in extinction figures would lead to some disagreement between the World Conservation Union and the Field Museum, but no. Just as the old revolutionary slogan was "No enemies on the left," so the present variant is "No environmental exaggeration is too great in a good cause." Indeed, the IUCN appears clearly frustrated that it is bounded by actual observed science in doing its godly environmental work. Its assumptions of invisible species loss is right up there with that of the Field, in fact, way out in front of it. Nevertheless, its "hard" figures, despite the hysterical spin put on them, suggest that the "biotic holocaust" is a myth. In a good cause, of course. Donate today.

Further requests for information from the Field eventually produced a reply from the scientist in charge of the extinction exhibit. He concluded, after appropriate citations from "the literature," that "the overwhelming consensus of scientists studying biodiversity around the world is that Earth is currently involved in a period of incredible species loss."

Incredible indeed.

6

Biodiversity Loss in the World's Oceans Threatens Human Well-Being

Communication Partnership for Science and the Sea

The Communication Partnership for Science and the Sea (COMPASS) is a collaborative effort of the conservation organization SeaWeb, the Monterey Bay Aquarium's Center for the Future of the Oceans, and academic scientists. COMPASS promotes marine conservation science and encourages immediate solutions to important marine environmental problems. One way COMPASS promotes marine conservation science is by giving voice to leading scientific efforts such as the results of the study outlined in the following press release.

A 2006 meta-study of worldwide research on ocean ecosystems concludes that biodiversity loss threatens the oceans' capacity to produce seafood and recover from the stresses caused by disease and pollutants. These global trends challenge the oceans' ability to feed the world's growing population. Biodiversity loss also makes coastal ecosystems vulnerable to invasive species that expose those who live in coastal regions to noxious algal blooms. However, the data also reveal that it may not be too late. Efforts to increase biodiversity such as managing fisheries, creating marine reserves, and controlling pollution may stem threats to the world's marine food supply.

Communication Partnership for Science and the Sea, "Accelerating Loss of Ocean Species Threatens Human Well-Being," SeaWeb, November 2, 2006. Reproduced by permission.

In a study published in the November 3 [2006] issue of the journal *Science*, an international group of ecologists and economists shows that the loss of biodiversity is profoundly reducing the ocean's ability to produce seafood, resist diseases, filter pollutants, and rebound from stresses such as over fishing and climate change. The study reveals that every species lost causes a faster unraveling of the overall ecosystem. Conversely every species recovered adds significantly to overall productivity and stability of the ecosystem and its ability to withstand stresses.

"Whether we looked at tide pools or studies over the entire world's ocean, we saw the same picture emerging," says lead author Boris Worm of Dalhousie University. "In losing species we lose the productivity and stability of entire ecosystems. I was shocked and disturbed by how consistent these trends are—beyond anything we suspected."

The four-year analysis is the first to examine all existing data on ocean species and ecosystems, synthesizing historical, experimental, fisheries, and observational datasets to understand the importance of biodiversity at the global scale.

Global Trends

The results reveal global trends that mirror what scientists have observed at smaller scales, and they prove that progressive biodiversity loss not only impairs the ability of oceans to feed a growing human population, but also sabotages the stability of marine environments and their ability to recover from stresses. Every species matters.

"For generations, people have admired the denizens of the sea for their size, ferocity, strength or beauty. But as this study shows, the animals and plants that inhabit the sea are not merely embellishments to be wondered at," says Callum Roberts, a Professor at the University of York, who was not involved in the study. "They are essential to the health of the oceans and the well-being of human society."

"This analysis provides the best documentation I have ever seen regarding biodiversity's value," adds Peter Kareiva, a former Brown University professor and US government fisheries manager who now leads science efforts at The Nature Conservancy. "There is no way the world will protect biodiversity without this type of compelling data demonstrating the economic value of biodiversity."

The current global trend ... projects the collapse of all species of wild seafood that are currently fished by the year 2050.

The good news is that the data show that ocean ecosystems still hold great ability to rebound. However, the current global trend is a serious concern: it projects the collapse of all species of wild seafood that are currently fished by the year 2050 (collapse is defined as 90% depletion).

Collapses are also hastened by the decline in overall health of the ecosystem—fish rely on the clean water, prey populations and diverse habitats that are linked to higher diversity systems. This points to the need for managers to consider all species together rather than continuing with single species management.

"Unless we fundamentally change the way we manage all the oceans' species together, as working ecosystems, then this century is the last century of wild seafood," says co-author Steve Palumbi of Stanford University.

The Impacts of Species Loss

The impacts of species loss go beyond declines in seafood. Human health risks emerge as depleted coastal ecosystems become vulnerable to invasive species, disease outbreaks and noxious algal blooms.

Many of the economic activities along our coasts rely on diverse systems and the healthy waters they supply. "The ocean is a great recycler," explains Palumbi, "It takes sewage and recycles it into nutrients, it scrubs toxins out of the water, and it produces food and turns carbon dioxide into food and oxygen." But in order to provide these services, the ocean needs all its working parts, the millions of plant and animal species that inhabit the sea.

The strength of the study is the consistent agreement of theory, experiments and observations across widely different scales and ecosystems. The study analyzed 32 controlled experiments, observational studies from 48 marine protected areas, and global catch data from the UN's [United Nations] Food and Agriculture Organization's (FAO) database of all fish and invertebrates worldwide from 1950 to 2003. The scientists also looked at a 1000-year time series for 12 coastal regions, drawing on data from archives, fishery records, sediment cores and archeological data.

"We see an accelerating decline in coastal species over the last 1000 years, resulting in the loss of biological filter capacity, nursery habitats, and healthy fisheries," says co-author Heike Lotze of Dalhousie University who led the historical analysis of Chesapeake Bay, San Francisco Bay, the Bay of Fundy, and the North Sea, among others.

Restoring marine biodiversity through an ecosystem based management approach . . . is essential to avoid serious threats to global food security, coastal water quality and ecosystem stability.

A Pressing Question

The scientists note that a pressing question for management is whether losses can be reversed. If species have not been pushed too far down, recovery can be fast—but there is also a point of no return as seen with species like northern Atlantic cod.

Examination of protected areas worldwide show that restoration of biodiversity increased productivity four-fold in terms of catch per unit effort and made ecosystems 21% less susceptible to environmental and human caused fluctuations on average.

"The data show us it's not too late," says Worm. "We can turn this around. But less than one percent of the global ocean is effectively protected right now. We won't see complete recovery in one year, but in many cases species come back more quickly than people anticipated—in three to five to ten years. And where this has been done we see immediate economic benefits."

The buffering impact of species diversity also generates long term insurance values that must be incorporated into future economic valuation and management decisions. "Although there are short-term economic costs associated with preservation of marine biodiversity, over the long term biodiversity conservation and economic development are complementary goals," says co-author Ed Barbier, an economist from the University of Wyoming.

The authors conclude that restoring marine biodiversity through an ecosystem based management approach—including integrated fisheries management, pollution control, maintenance of essential habitats and creation of marine reserves—is essential to avoid serious threats to global food security, coastal water quality and ecosystem stability.

"This isn't predicted to happen, this is happening now," says co-author Nicola Beaumont, an ecological economist with the Plymouth Marine Laboratory. "If biodiversity continues to decline, the marine environment will not be able to sustain our way of life, indeed it may not be able to sustain our lives at all."

7

Exaggerated Claims of Biodiversity Loss Lead to Poor Solutions

Bjørn Lomborg

Danish author and academic Bjørn Lomborg organized the Copenhagen Consensus to establish priorities for advancing global welfare based on what its members argue are rational methodologies, rather than those based on the "court of public opinion." Lomborg is adjunct professor at the Copenhagen Business School and author of the controversial books Cool It *and* The Skeptical Environmentalist.

Global warming activists are using the allure of polar bears in a misguided effort to generate support for expensive policies that will do little to save the bears or improve human welfare. Of the world's polar bears, most populations are stable—only two are actually at risk. Focusing on poachers, not greenhouse gases, would better protect the bears. Environmental policy makers should provide people with the truth, including the fact that warming temperatures actually will improve life for many species. Indeed, the goal of environmental policies should be to improve life for all creatures that inhabit the Earth, including humans.

A forlorn polar bear stands wistfully on a melting iceberg. This evocative image brings to life the threat of global warming. At least, that's what the editors of *Time* magazine thought.

Bjørn Lomborg, "The No-So-Disappearing Polar Bear," *Telegraph* (UK), October 16, 2007. Copyright © Telegraph Media Group Limited 2007. Reproduced by permission.

A polar bear was their choice for the cover of a climate change-themed issue, along with the warning: "Be worried. Be very worried".

Former US vice president and Nobel Peace Prize winner Al Gore says melting ice is causing polar bears to drown.

The *Independent* newspaper believes polar bears will soon be found only in zoos, while the World Wildlife Fund predicts they will be unable to reproduce within five years.

The polar bear is being used to spur the world to take drastic action against climate change. Facts derail this call to arms. This is the climate change scare writ small.

Media-Assisted Hysteria

In the 1960s, there were probably 5,000 polar bears around the globe. Forty years later—thanks largely to a reduction in hunting—the World Conservation Union (IUCN) counts five-times that many.

The world's 25,000 polar bears live in 20 distinct populations. Two populations are growing. Most are stable. Just two are waning.

The declining populations are in areas that have gotten colder over the past 50 years. The habitats of the two thriving groups have actually become warmer.

It is important not to let cute pin-up 'victims' crowd out the facts.

If polar bears are today's 'canaries in the coalmine' then the coalmine does not appear half as fearsome as some claim.

Al Gore bases his claim of "drowning" bears on a single sighting of four dead bears the day after an abrupt windstorm. The sighting occurred in an area where polar bear numbers are increasing.

Last year a Canadian polar bear specialist summed up the difference between the facts and the hype: "It is just silly to predict the demise of polar bears in 25 years based on media-assisted hysteria."

This doesn't mean polar bears will escape man-made global warming. Disappearing ice will eventually make their life more difficult. They are likely to adapt and become more like the brown bears from which they evolved. Their numbers could decline, although a dramatic drop appears unlikely.

As I argue in my new book *Cool It* coming out this autumn [2007], we can learn two lessons about the climate change debate from the tale of the vanishing polar bears.

First, it is important not to let cute pin-up 'victims' crowd out the facts. We care about the entire environment, not just polar bears. Many creatures and plants in the Arctic will actually do better as temperatures rise.

The Arctic ecosystem will experience greater species richness and higher productivity. There will be more nesting birds and butterflies. Those don't make up for waning populations of polar bears, but we need to hear both sides of the story.

The case of the not-so-vanishing polar bears shows that we shouldn't let the smartest solutions get lost amid the hype.

Second, it's easy to let misplaced fear guide us the wrong way.

Campaigners like Gore usually base their claims about 'vanishing' polar bears on observations of just one population. This well-studied group in Canada's western Hudson Bay did decline from 1,200 in 1987 to fewer than 950 in 2004.

But back in the early 1980s, the population numbered just 500. In other words, it's actually doubled over two decades. The much-publicised 'decline' depends on when you start counting.

For the sake of peace, let's accept the idea that we should base our view of the world's entire polar bear population on the fluctuations in this one group. Let's even allow the problematic notion that we should start counting those bears at their height in 1987. Based on these assumptions, we are losing 15 bears a year to climate change.

That means that we could save 15 bears each year if we could stop global warming right now. Of course, we can't. The Kyoto Protocol[1] will cost $180 billion dollars, yet do almost no good: it would save just 0.06 polar bear each year.

Looking for Smarter Options

There are dramatically smarter options available if we care about polar bears. Hunters shoot 49 bears from western Hudson Bay each year. For each bear we save with climate change policies, we could save 260 by revoking hunting rights and clamping down on poachers.

That's the approach favoured by the IUCN (the World Conservation Union). But we don't hear a lot about that.

In fact, we seldom hear about the smartest solutions to climate change. We should make a 10-fold increase in research to make zero-carbon energy cheaper in the future. This would be much more efficient than Kyoto, yet cost almost 10 times less.

We have lost sight of our goal. We hear an awful lot about how to cut greenhouse gas emissions but our overall aim is not to reduce gasses but to improve life for humans and our planet.

The case of the not-so-vanishing polar bears shows that we shouldn't let the smartest solutions get lost amid the hype.

---

1. The Kyoto Protocol is a United Nations protocol aimed at combating global warming. Those who ratify the treaty agree to reduce greenhouses gas emissions. As of October 2009, 184 nations have signed and ratified the protocol. The United States, responsible for 36.1 percent of emissions in 1990 has signed, but has not ratified the protocol.

8

Global Warming Threatens Biodiversity

David A. Fahrenthold

David A. Fahrenthold, a staff writer for the Washington Post, *often writes about environmental issues, frequently those that involve the communities of Washington, DC, and Maryland.*

Mechanisms such as evolution and migration, which helped plants and animals survive climate changes in the past, are ineffective in the face of today's rapid global warming. Indeed, current global warming trends pose a serious threat to biodiversity. Rapid melting of Arctic ice has severely reduced the hunting grounds of polar bears, and rising sea levels eliminate habitat for other animals. Migrating birds, confused by climate change, arrive too early to find inadequate food. While some animals will indeed thrive in a warmer climate, this news offers little comfort to those species that will not survive and the people who value these creatures.

What has gone missing here [in the Blackwater National Wildlife Refuge in Maryland] is almost as spectacular as the 8,000 acres of swampy wilderness that remain. And that makes it Chesapeake Bay's best place to watch climate change in action.

Visitors can see ospreys gliding overhead, egrets wading in the channels and Delmarva fox squirrels making their unhurried commutes between pine trees.

David A. Fahrenthold, "Climate Change Brings Risk of More Extinctions," *Washington Post*, September 17, 2007. Copyright © 2007, The Washington Post. Reprinted with permission.

But then the road turns a corner, and Blackwater's marsh yields to a vast expanse of open water. This is what's missing: There used to be thousands more acres of wetland here, providing crucial habitat for creatures including blue crabs and blue herons. But, thanks in part to rising sea levels, it has drowned and become a large, salty lake. "If people want to see the effects" of Earth's increasing temperature, refuge biologist Roger Stone said, "it's happening here first."

Altering Natural Ecosystems

But not just here. Around the world, scientists have found that climate change is altering natural ecosystems, making profound changes in the ways that animals live, migrate, eat and grow. Some species have benefited from the shift. Others have been left disastrously out of sync with their food supply. Two are known to have simply disappeared.

If warming continues as predicted, scientists say, 20 percent or more of the planet's plant and animal species could be at increased risk of extinction. But, as the shrinking habitat at Blackwater shows, the bad news isn't all in the out years: Some changes have already begun. "This is actually something we see from pole to pole, and from sea level to the highest mountains in the world," said Lara Hansen, chief climate change scientist at the World Wildlife Fund, a private research and advocacy group. "It is not something we're going to see in the future. It's something we see right now."

The temperature increase behind these changes sounds slight. The world has been getting warmer by 0.2 degrees Fahrenheit every decade, a U.N. [United Nations] panel found this year, in part because of carbon dioxide and other human-generated gases that trap heat in Earth's atmosphere.

By nature's clock, the warming has come in an instant. The mechanisms that helped animals adapt during previous warming spells—evolution or long-range migration—often aren't able to keep up. Scientists say that effects are beginning to show from the Arctic to the Appalachian Mountains. One study, which examined 1,598 plant and animal species, found that nearly 60 percent appeared to have changed in some way.

"Even when animals don't go extinct, we're affecting them. They're going to be different than they were before," said David Skelly, a Yale University professor who has tracked frogs' ability to react to increasing warmth. "The fact that we're doing a giant evolutionary experiment should not be comforting," he said.

Problems Near the Poles

Some of the best-known changes are happening near the poles, where the air and the water are warming especially quickly. As they do, sea ice is receding. For some animals, this has meant literally the loss of the ground beneath their feet.

Polar bears, for instance, spend much of their life on the Arctic ice and use it as a hunting ground for seals. When ice on Canada's western Hudson Bay began to break up earlier—three weeks earlier in 2004 than in 1974—the effect was devastating. The bear population fell by 21 percent in 17 years. Shrinking ice has also been blamed for cannibalism among polar bears in the waters off Alaska, something scientists had not seen before 2004. This month, a U.S. Geological Survey report predicted that two-thirds of the world's polar bears could die out in 50 years.

Walruses, too, rely on the ice; mothers stash their calves on it, then dive down to feed on the ocean floor. When ice recedes from prime feeding areas, mothers and calves can get separated.

In 2004, University of Tennessee professor Lee W. Cooper was off the north Alaskan coast when he saw about a dozen calves swimming toward his boat. His theory: The calves, alone and desperate without ice nearby, thought the boat might be a large iceberg.

There was nothing the scientists could do to help, Cooper said. "I think they were doomed."

Shifting Patterns

Other changes have been less deadly, but they show centuries-old patterns shifting. Scientists have noticed changes in the timing of seasonal migrations, presumably caused by the earlier onset of warm weather.

In some cases, migrating animals suddenly find themselves out of rhythm, missing the weather conditions or the food they need. In parts of the Rocky Mountains, American robins arrive two weeks earlier than they used to—and often discover the ground snow-covered and little food to be found.

In other cases, an animal's entire territory shifts as old habitats become too warm. In many cases, this means a move north. In others, it means a move up.

The American pika, a small rodent that lives on the slopes of mountains in the western United States, can overheat when temperatures hit 80 degrees. Over the past century, these creatures have kept climbing, reaching new ranges that can be 1,300 feet up the slope.

In some cases, there is no escape. In Costa Rica's Monteverde Cloud Forest, a famous region that is kept damp by fog and mist, climate change has brought more variable weather and less of the clouds that some animals need.

Two amphibian species—the golden toad and the Monteverde harlequin frog—have not been seen since the late 1980s. These may be some of the first extinctions linked to climate change, said cloud forest researcher Alan Pounds. "It's been an interesting puzzle to work on," Pounds said. "But, at the same time, very alarming and frightening."

Melting at the Marsh

At the Blackwater refuge, it is rising waters, not rising temperatures, that are eliminating habitat. A quirk of geology means that water rises especially fast here: Paradoxically, the land in this area is sinking as North America slowly unbends from the weight of glaciers during the last ice age.

Add that to the effect of melting polar ice, and scientists expect that most of the marsh will become open water by 2030. When it goes, there could be a shortage of habitat for the Eastern Shore's marsh animals and migratory birds, said Stone, the refuge biologist.

"Birds will return for spring migration, and they'll be looking for territory, and there just won't be enough territory to go around," he said.

So what happens then?

"They'll ..." he paused, looking for the right word, "... die. They'll disappear."

Not all animals, of course, will suffer. There are examples of creatures that are thriving in a warmer world. Fish such as pollock and pink salmon have begun moving into now-warmer Arctic waters. In the northern woods of North America, some tick species are making it through the winter in record numbers.

Climate change will not be bad for all animals. . . . Cold comfort for the rest—and for humans . . . if it means that we watch some of the planet's most beloved species decline or disappear.

Livestock herds might increase in a warmer world, an analysis by the Agriculture Department found. That's because food crops such as corn and rice could become harder to grow if the fields dry out, leaving more land for grazing. Researchers say that, even if all greenhouse-gas emissions were shut off today, the gases already in the atmosphere will cause Earth to warm for years to come. But, many say, it's still imperative to reduce these emissions to head off even more warming.

Turning the Supertanker Around

"Unfortunately, it takes a generation or two to turn this supertanker around," said Stephen Schneider, a professor at Stanford University, talking about the climate change already in progress. But still, he said, it is important to start trying. "What we're looking at is a planetary environmental train wreck if we don't start some compromising here."

Already, some are trying to make it easier for wild animals to adjust. In Australia, conservationists are trying to set aside a north-south cordon of open land so animals can move if they need to. In the western United States and Canada, environmentalists are trying to create a similar corridor between Yellowstone National Park and the Yukon Territory.

Overall, scientists say, the news of climate change will not be bad for all animals. But, they say, that's cold comfort for the rest—and for humans, as well, if it means that we watch some of the planet's most beloved species decline or disappear.

"Yeah, the earth will recover," said Scott Wing, who studies the biology of previous eras at the Smithsonian Institution. But, he said, "would you have wanted to be one of the dinosaurs when the asteroid hit? No."

9

Global Warming Does Not Threaten Biodiversity

Daniel B. Botkin

Daniel B. Botkin, president of the Center for the Study of the Environment and professor emeritus in the Department of Ecology, Evolution, and Marine Biology at the University of California, Santa Barbara, is the author of Discordant Harmonies: A New Ecology for the Twenty-First Century.

Evidence does not support claims that global warming poses a serious threat to biodiversity. In fact, the opposite is true. During similar warming periods over the last 2.5 million years, few species became extinct. Moreover, studies show that global warming does not increase disease. In fact, some species, including humans, thrived during historical warming periods. Unfortunately, focusing conservation efforts on reducing global warming does put biodiversity at risk, by diverting funds that would be better spent reducing habitat loss, one of the gravest threats to biodiversity.

Global warming doesn't matter except to the extent that it will affect life—ours and that of all living things on Earth. And contrary to the latest news, the evidence that global warming will have serious effects on life is thin. Most evidence suggests the contrary.

Contrary Evidence

Case in point: This year's United Nations report on climate change and other documents say that 20% to 30% of plant and animal species will be threatened with extinction in this century due to global warming—a truly terrifying thought. Yet, during the past 2.5 million years, a period that scientists now know experienced climatic changes as rapid and as warm as modern climatological models suggest will happen to us, almost none of the millions of species on Earth went extinct. The exceptions were about 20 species of large mammals (the famous megafauna of the last ice age—saber-tooth tigers, hairy mammoths and the like), which went extinct about 10,000 to 5,000 years ago at the end of the last ice age, and many dominant trees and shrubs of northwestern Europe. But elsewhere, including North America, few plant species went extinct, and few mammals.

We're also warned that tropical diseases are going to spread, and that we can expect malaria and encephalitis epidemics. But scientific papers by Prof. Sarah Randolph of Oxford University show that temperature changes do not correlate well with changes in the distribution or frequency of these diseases; warming has not broadened their distribution and is highly unlikely to do so in the future, global warming or not.

The key point here is that living things respond to many factors in addition to temperature and rainfall. In most cases, however, climate-modeling-based forecasts look primarily at temperature alone, or temperature and precipitation only. You might ask, "Isn't this enough to forecast changes in the distribution of species?" Ask a mockingbird. *The New York Times* recently published an answer to a query about why mockingbirds were becoming common in Manhattan. The expert answer was: food—an exotic plant species that mockingbirds like to eat had spread to New York City. It was this, not temperature or rainfall, the expert said, that caused the change in mockingbird geography.

Belief in the Scientific Method

You might think I must be one of those know-nothing nay-sayers who believes global warming is a liberal plot. On the contrary, I am a biologist and ecologist who has worked on global warming, and been concerned about its effects, since 1968. I've developed the computer model of forest growth that has been used widely to forecast possible effects of global warming on life—I've used the model for that purpose myself, and to forecast likely effects on specific endangered species.

I'm not a naysayer. I'm a scientist who believes in the scientific method and in what facts tell us. I have worked for 40 years to try to improve our environment and improve human life as well. I believe we can do this only from a basis in reality, and that is not what I see happening now. Instead, like fashions that took hold in the past and are eloquently analyzed in the classic 19th century book *Extraordinary Popular Delusions and the Madness of Crowds*, the popular imagination today appears to have been captured by beliefs that have little scientific basis.

Some colleagues who share some of my doubts argue that the only way to get our society to change is to frighten people with the possibility of a catastrophe, and that therefore it is all right and even necessary for scientists to exaggerate. They tell me that my belief in open and honest assessment is naïve. "Wolves deceive their prey, don't they?" one said to me recently. Therefore, biologically, he said, we are justified in exaggerating to get society to change.

The climate modelers who developed the computer programs that are being used to forecast climate change used to readily admit that the models were crude and not very realistic, but were the best that could be done with available computers and programming methods. They said our options were to either believe those crude models or believe the opinions of experienced, data-focused scientists. Having done a great deal of computer modeling myself, I appreciated their acknowledgment of the limits of their methods. But I hear no such statements today. Oddly, the forecasts of computer models have become our new reality, while facts such as the few extinctions of the past 2.5 million years are pushed aside, as if they were not our reality.

A recent article in the well-respected journal *American Scientist* explained why the glacier on Mt. Kilimanjaro could not be melting from global warming. Simply from an intellectual point of view it was fascinating—especially the author's Sherlock Holmes approach to figuring out what was causing the glacier to melt. That it couldn't be global warming directly (i.e., the result of air around the glacier warming) was made clear by the fact that the air temperature at the altitude of the glacier is below freezing. This means that only direct radiant heat from sunlight could be warming and melting the glacier. The author also studied the shape of the glacier and deduced that its melting pattern was consistent with radiant heat but not air temperature. Although acknowledged by many scientists, the paper is scorned by the true believers in global warming.

Not everything due to a climatic warming is bad, nor is everything that is bad due to a climatic warming.

Looking at Other Warmings

We are told that the melting of the arctic ice will be a disaster. But during the famous medieval warming period—A.D. 750 to 1230 or so—the Vikings found the warmer northern climate to their advantage. Emmanuel Le Roy Ladurie addressed this in his book *Times of Feast, Times of Famine: A History of Climate Since the Year 1000,* perhaps the greatest book about climate change before the onset of modern concerns with global warming. He wrote that Erik the Red "took advantage of a sea relatively free of ice to sail due west from Iceland to reach

Greenland. . . . Two and a half centuries later, at the height of the climatic and demographic fortunes of the northern settlers, a bishopric of Greenland was founded at Gardar in 1126."

Ladurie pointed out that "it is reasonable to think of the Vikings as unconsciously taking advantage of this [referring to the warming of the Middle Ages] to colonize the most northern and inclement of their conquests, Iceland and Greenland." Good thing that Erik the Red didn't have Al Gore or his climatologists as his advisers.

Making a Realistic Assessment

Should we therefore dismiss global warming? Of course not. But we should make a realistic assessment, as rationally as possible, about its cultural, economic and environmental effects. As Erik the Red might have told you, not everything due to a climatic warming is bad, nor is everything that is bad due to a climatic warming.

We should approach the problem the way we decide whether to buy insurance and take precautions against other catastrophes—wildfires, hurricanes, earthquakes. And as I have written elsewhere, many of the actions we would take to reduce greenhouse-gas production and mitigate global-warming effects are beneficial anyway, most particularly a movement away from fossil fuels to alternative solar and wind energy.

My concern is that we may be moving away from an irrational lack of concern about climate change to an equally irrational panic about it.

Many of my colleagues ask, "What's the problem? Hasn't it been a good thing to raise public concern?" The problem is that in this panic we are going to spend our money unwisely, we will take actions that are counterproductive, and we will fail to do many of those things that will benefit the environment and ourselves.

For example, right now the clearest threat to many species is habitat destruction. Take the orangutans, for instance, one of those charismatic species that people are often fascinated by and concerned about. They are endangered because of deforestation. In our fear of global warming, it would be sad if we fail to find funds to purchase those forests before they are destroyed, and thus let this species go extinct.

At the heart of the matter is how much faith we decide to put in science—even how much faith scientists put in science. Our times have benefited from clear-thinking, science-based rationality. I hope this prevails as we try to deal with our changing climate.

10

Bioprospecting Poses a Threat to Biodiversity and Indigenous Populations

Vandana Shiva

Vandana Shiva, born in India to a father who was a farmer and conservator of forests, is a physicist, feminist, economic/ environmental activist, and author. Among her many activist causes, Shiva has fought to protect biodiversity and indigenous intellectual property rights.

Bioprospecting, the commercialization of indigenous knowledge such as the medicinal use of plant and animal life, is simply biopiracy in disguise. Turning indigenous knowledge into intellectual property and biodiversity into raw materials to be exploited threatens biological and cultural diversity. Diverting biological resources to greedy private interests leads to scarcity in local communities and extinction of species. Claims that bioprospecting improves the lives of poor, indigenous communities are false. In fact, bioprospecting creates poverty in these communities by creating monopolies on resources that once met the community's food and health needs. To protect cultural and biological diversity, indigenous communities must reclaim their knowledge.

B ioprospecting is a term that was created in response to the problematic relationship between global commercial interests and the biological resources and indigenous knowledge of

Vandana Shiva, "Bioprospecting as Sophisticated Biopiracy," *Signs: Journal of Women in Culture and Society*, vol. 32, 2007, pp. 307–313. Copyright © 2007 University of Chicago Press. All rights reserved. Reproduced by permission of the University of Chicago Press, conveyed through Copyright Clearance Center, Inc.

local communities—and to the epidemic of biopiracy, the patenting of indigenous knowledge related to biodiversity. Bioprospecting was first defined by Walter V. Reid et al. as "the exploration of biodiversity for commercially valuable genetic resources and biochemicals" (1993, 1). Bioprospecting is an inappropriate term and an inappropriate process. It is derived from prospecting for minerals and fossil fuels. However, unlike fossil fuels, living resources are not useless unless exploited by global commercial interests for global markets. Biodiversity is the basis of living cultures. It is the foundation of the living economies of two-thirds of humanity, who depend on biodiversity for their livelihoods and needs.

Bioprospecting is viewed commercially as the exploration of potentially profitable biodiversity and biodiversity-related knowledge. However, biodiversity and indigenous knowledge are the basis of living economies and living cultures. Biodiversity and cultural diversity mutually conserve and shape each other. Viewed by indigenous communities, bioprospecting is seen as an expropriation of their collective and cumulative innovation, which they have utilized, protected, and conserved since time immemorial.

The very concept of bioprospecting is legally flawed since it is based on patenting traditional knowledge. A patent is granted for inventions, which must be novel. Existing knowledge—the product of thousands of years of collective innovation by indigenous cultures—is not an invention.

Bioprospecting creates impoverishment within donor communities by claiming monopolies on resources and knowledge that previously enabled communities to meet their health and nutrition needs and by forcing those communities to pay for what was originally theirs. Thus bioprospecting leads to the enclosure of the biological and intellectual commons through the conversion of indigenous communities' usurped biodiversity and biodiversity-related knowledge into commodities protected by intellectual property rights (IPRs).

How Bioprospecting Undermines Access

Bioprospecting is being promoted as a model for relationships between corporations, which commercialize indigenous knowledge, and indigenous communities, which have collectively developed the knowledge. It is being presented as an alternative to biopiracy. However, bioprospecting is merely a sophisticated form of biopiracy.

Collective innovation, evolving over time and involving many persons, is different from individual innovation, which is localized in time and space. Collective innovation is modified and enhanced as it is used over time and passed on from generation to generation. In some instances collective innovation is no longer local, for example, in the case of seeds and in the case of major non-Western knowledge traditions such as ayurvedic and Chinese medicine. In some cases it even crosses national boundaries.

This is particularly so with *ayahuasca*, which means vine of the soul, a plant used to make an intoxicating drink manufactured for ritual healing and enlightenment. Traditional stories about the origins of this powerful tonic weave together ancestral guidance, communication with the spirits of the plants, and protection by visible and invisible guardians. Known by a variety of names, including *caapi, yahe, sainto daime,* and *ayahuasca,* the drink is produced using the bark of the jaguba vine (*Banisteriopsis caapi*).

Transnational corporations have posed a potential threat to the biological and intellectual heritage of our diverse communities by appropriating and privatizing their knowledge.

An American citizen, Loren Miller, obtained a U.S. patent for a variety of *Banisteriopsis caapi* that he had collected from an indigenous person's garden. He dubbed the *ayahuasca* plant "Da Vine." The bioprospecting/biopiracy patent was challenged by the coordinating body of indigenous organizations of the Amazon Basin (Coordinadora de las Organizaciones Indígenas de la Cuenca Amazónica, or COICA), an umbrella group that represents 400 indigenous tribes in the region. The challenge led to the subsequent rejection of Miller's patent claim in November 1999 (Shuler 2004, 169–70).

Another case of bioprospecting that has been cited as a success story of benefit sharing by the global community but that is viewed as a failure by the indigenous community is the case of *arogya pacha*, or jeevan, a plant that the Kaui tribe has used to treat fatigue and stress. This plant was commercialized through a contract between the Tropical Botanical Garden Research Institute of Trivandrum and a pharmaceutical company. A U.S. company, Nutri Science Innovations, is selling the drug online. The estimated market value is $1 billion; the Kaui community received only $12,000 (Varshney 2004).

The biological diversity of India has always been a common resource for our traditional communities, which have utilized, protected, and conserved their biodiversity heritage over centuries. Their collective and cumulative innovation has been the basis of local culture and local economies, which constitute the dominant economies in terms of the livelihoods provided and the needs met. In fact, their traditional knowledge in medicine, agriculture, and fisheries is the primary base for meeting their food and health needs. For them, conserving biodiversity means conserving the integrity of the ecosystem and species, the right to resources and knowledge, and the right to the production systems based on biodiversity. Therefore, biodiversity is intimately linked to traditional indigenous knowledge systems as well as to people's rights to protect their knowledge and resources.

However, nature's diversity and the diversity of knowledge systems are undergoing a major process of destabilization with the expansion of patents and IPRs into the domain of biodiversity via the Trade-Related Aspects of Intellectual Property Rights (TRIPs) agreement of the World Trade Organization. The whole notion of TRIPs has been shaped by the objectives and interests of trade and transnational corporations. Through the instrument of TRIPs, transnational corporations have posed a potential threat to the biological and intellectual heritage of our diverse communities by appropriating and privatizing their knowledge. For these commercial interests, biodiversity itself has no value; it is merely a raw material for the production of commodities and for the maximization of profits. In the context of privatization, the mutual exchange among communities has been replaced by contracts for bioprospecting by corporations that seek to expropriate the invaluable and inalienable heritage of communities, often through scientific collection missions and ethnobotanical research.

The metaphor of prospecting is borrowed from the practice of prospecting for gold or oil. While biodiversity is fast becoming green gold or green oil for the pharmaceutical and biotechnology industries, the metaphor of prospecting suggests that prior to prospecting the resources lie buried, unknown, unused, and without value. However, unlike the case with gold or oil deposits, local communities know the uses and value of biodiversity. The metaphor of bioprospecting thus hides the prior uses, knowledge, and rights associated with it. Taking knowledge from indigenous communities through bioprospecting is only the first step in developing an IPR-protected industrial system that markets commodities that have been developed through local knowledge but are not based on the ethical, epistemological, or ecological structures of that knowledge system. Transnational corporations use biodiversity fragments as raw material to produce biological products protected by patents that displace the biodiversity and indigenous knowledge they have exploited. Bioprospecting is the first step toward establishing a dominant system of monocultures and monopolies, and thus accepting the destruction of diversity.

Indigenous knowledge is centered on interrelations between nature and people. Intellectual property rights regimes are premised on the denial of the creativity of nature. The ethical and epistemological assumptions and consequences of adopting an IPR regime through bioprospecting contracts need deeper analysis and reflection. This is particularly important since biodiversity knowledge in indigenous communities is not an individual but a collective innovation, not a privatized but a shared heritage. Therefore, all members of the community, including past generations, have contributed to the innovation, with many communities utilizing the knowledge and sharing the biological resources.

Bioprospecting usually involves a corporation sending an ethnoscientist to talk to a member of an indigenous community and to settle on compensation with the individual or the community. However, other communities will feel the impact of this transaction in the future. The utilization of biodiversity in the people's economy is guided by a plurality of knowledge systems. Local communities understand the implementation of the properties, characteristics, and uses of this biodiversity in different languages and in diverse epistemological frameworks. Suppose that other communities do not support the privatization of this common heritage. Bioprospecting has no room for respecting the rights of people and communities who do not want their common genetic resources enclosed. It is for those who do not accept the inevitability of the enclosure of our biodiversity that the alternatives to bioprospecting become an imperative.

In the case of a resource such as land, which cannot be multiplied, land-based commons have clear territorial boundaries for communities that have access to common forests or pastures. Communities have very strict limits on resource use. The exploitation of these commons will only go as far as the subsistence level so communities cannot limitlessly exploit the commons for private gains. The principles and rules of management of the commons set strict upper limits so no one can exploit too much and lower limits so no individual in the community is excluded from utilizing the commons. In the case of agricultural resources and knowledge, which multiply by sharing and do not intrinsically reduce the givers' share, the community of uses is always expanding. Thus, seeds travel across communities, increasing their uses and innovations, becoming available to all communities that have shared their biological and intellectual contributions.

The bioprospecting paradigm needs to be examined in the context of equity, specifically its effect on the donor community, potential recipient communities, and bioprospecting corporations. Even though bioprospecting contracts are based on prior informed consent and compensation, unlike the case of biopiracy where no consent is taken and no compensation given, not all owners/carriers of an indigenous knowledge tradition are consulted or compensated. Not only does this lead to inequity and injustice but it also has the potential of pitting individual against individual within a community and community against community. For example, an innovation might have been developed by a group of communities. A bioprospecting contract enables a corporation to seize this collective knowledge by signing a contract with one community. This contract violates the biodiversity and knowledge rights of all other communities that hold the knowledge and resources in common with the community that signed the contract.

For this reason the bioprospecting model—which deals with one individual, one community, or one interest group—can never be equitable. A commercial interest needs to get informed consent from all communities and all members of each community who have used and contributed to collective innovation in biodiversity-related knowledge. In the case of biodiversity-related collective innovation there are many interests involved: farmers and the seed industry, traditional healers and pharmaceutical corporations, Western and non-

Western scientific traditions, and masculinist ways of knowing and feminist ways of knowing. All the diverse communities of interest have to be included in a transaction.

Collective rights cannot be abjured or relinquished by any one community of users, by any individual member of any community, or by the state on behalf of any community. The bioprospecting model, therefore, is not a legitimate source of benefit sharing. It is based on a double exclusion. The first exclusion takes place when communities of users/innovators are excluded, when one group is treated as holding the knowledge exclusively. The second exclusion takes place when the commercial enterprise signing a bioprospecting contract takes an IPR on the knowledge transferred from an indigenous community as an unjustified claim to innovation. Over time this excludes the donor community itself as marketing systems and IPR regimes combine to make the community that provided biological resources and knowledge dependent on purchasing proprietary commodities from the corporations that monopolize the biodiversity and knowledge. For example, farmers who contributed seed in a bioprospecting venture are forced to buy proprietary seed from the seed industry.

How Bioprospecting Creates Poverty

Bioprospecting is often presented as a means for making the poor rich. It is often stated that the biodiversity-rich regions are financially poor and since bioprospecting is associated with monetary compensation, bioprospecting can make biodiversity-rich regions financially rich as well. However, the bioprospecting model is a model for taking away the last resources, both natural and intellectual, from the poor. It is therefore in reality a model for creating poverty for the community as a whole even when it might bring money to a few individuals in that community.

The poverty-creating impact of biopiracy and bioprospecting can only be perceived if one recognizes that there is a difference between the material economy and the financial economy. On the one hand, if people have rich biodiversity and intellectual wealth, they can meet their needs for health care and nutrition through their own resources and their knowledge. If, on the other hand, the rights to both resources and knowledge have been transferred from the community to IPR holders, the members of the community end up paying high royalties for what was originally theirs and which they had for free. They therefore become materially poor.

Some communities are local users, and others are nonlocal users. Suppose that a community engages in a bioprospecting contact with a corporation and the corporation takes an IPR on products of the community's medicinal plant. The first impact is that all the other communities in the bioregion no longer have access to the seed or medicine they have used; they become poorer in nutrition and health terms. The second impact is that the communities become poorer in financial terms since they have to buy the seeds, agrochemicals, or medicines that they once derived freely from local plants' biodiversity.

When a corporation takes the biodiversity knowledge of a community, commercializes it, and transforms it into proprietary knowledge protected by IPRs, a number of impacts are felt by the donor community. As the products of biodiversity (e.g., medicinal plants) gain commercial value globally, they are exploited. It leads to diversion of the biological resource from meeting local needs to feeding nonlocal greed. This in turn generates scarcity, leading to price increases. In the case of overexploitation, it can lead to extinction. The local scarcity combined with IPRs on derived commodities eventually takes the resource and its products beyond the access of the donor communities, for example, in the case of the neem tree. Thus, the providing communities lose their rightful share to emerging markets. Other poor communities, whose traditions permit them to rely on free exchange or low-cost seeds and who could have received the knowledge for free or at low cost, are also made dependent on the commercial interest.

The bioprospecting perspective reflects the commodification and privatization paradigm, which only protects the rights of those who appropriate people's common resources and turn them into commodities. As I discuss above, the benefits provided and shared by indigenous and local communities are rendered invisible; the focus is only on the benefits shared by those who privatize and enclose the commons. Bioprospecting is sophisticated biopiracy, and its impact on biodiversity and indigenous cultures and local economies is the same as outright biopiracy. Reclaiming the intellectual commons through asserting collective intellectual property rights represents the real model of equitable benefit sharing since only the commons ensures equity and sharing.

References

1. Reid, Walter V., Sarah A. Laird, Rodrigo Gámez, Ana Sittenfeld, Daniel H. Janzen, Michael A. Gollin, and Calestous Juma, 1993. "A New Lease on Life." In *Biodiversity Prospecting: Using Genetic Resources for Sustainable Development*, ed. Walter V. Reid, Sarah A. Laird, Carrie A. Meyer, Rodrigo Gámez, Ana Sitenfeld, Daniel H. Janzen, Michael A. Gollin, and Calestous Juma, 1–52. Washington, DC: World Resources Institute.

2. Shuler, Philip, 2004. "Biopiracy and Commericalization of Ethnobotanical Knowledge." In *Poor People's Knowledge: Promoting Intellectual Property in Developing Countries*, ed. J. Michael Finger and Philip Schuler, 159–81. Washington, DC: World Bank and Oxford University Press.

3. Varshney, Vibha, 2004. "Tragic Potion: Tribals Lose Out as Herbal Drug Is Stuck in IPR Jam." *Down to Earth: Science and Environment Online* 12. http://www.downtoearth.org.in/full6.asp?foldername=20040331=news&sec_id=4&sid=18.

11

A Middle Ground Should Be Sought in Bioprospecting

David A. Dickson

David A. Dickson is director of the Science and Development Network, an organization whose mission is to explore how science and technology can reduce poverty, improve health, and raise standards of living, particularly in the developing world. Dickson has written on science and environmental issues for respected science journals such as Nature, Science, *and* New Scientist *since the early 1970s.*

The commercial motives behind scientific expeditions to study life in developing nations inevitably leads to fears that these biological resources will be exploited. To mediate these fears, scientists who study life in developing nations and conservationists who hope to protect native plant and animal life should collaborate to protect biodiversity. Conservationists must understand that overzealous rules and regulations can frustrate the legitimate pursuit of scientific knowledge that benefits conservation. Scientists, however, must accept that abuses by other scientists set the stage for rigorous laws to protect biodiversity. When scientists and conservationists recognize their mutual interests, both sides win.

Scientists have long been implicated, whether actively or tacitly, in developed countries' campaigns to seek out and secure natural resources to fuel industrialisation and maintain their own living standards.

David A. Dickson, "Biopiracy Requires Reasoned Treatment," Science and Development Network, September 14, 2007, Editorials. Copyright © 2007 SciDev.Net. Reproduced by permission.

This was the motive behind many 'scientific' expeditions to explore and map out the centre of Africa in the 19th century. More recently, studying indigenous medicine has become a cost-effective way of identifying active chemical ingredients from plants that might be valuable in modern medicine.

Inevitably, as the commercial and economic motivations behind such 'scientific' enterprises emerge, resentment grows at the perceived one-way flow of benefits. In response, strongly worded commitments to enforcing greater social justice are developed. The most influential of these is the Convention on Biological Diversity (CBD), which came into force in 1993, giving states ownership, and thus control, over the plants and animals within their borders.

Equally inevitably, efforts to implement such commitments have frequently generated protest from scientists. They miss their previous freedom to collect, transport and disseminate research samples virtually at will, and view the requirements for permits and prior approval as a mire of red tape that frequently delays projects.

A Wave of Protest

The recent imprisonment of a Dutch-born researcher, Marc van Roosmalen, who has been working in the Brazilian rainforest for more than 20 years and whose work has helped name several newly identified species of primates, has been a focus for scientists' anger.

Van Roosmalen previously worked for the National Institute for Research in the Amazon in Manaus, in the heart of Amazonia, but now runs his own private research institution. In June [2007] he was sentenced to almost 16 years in prison for infringing laws introduced to protect Brazil's treasure trove of natural resources.

His treatment triggered a wave of protest from scientists, both in Brazil and, eventually, internationally. For many scientists the case symbolises what they see as the unfair victimisation of the scientific community by those seeking to preserve natural environments at any cost.

The Association for Tropical Biology and Conservation Scientists, for example, officially described van Roosmalen's treatment as a government-backed "attack on the practice and profession of biological scientists", and called for his immediate release. The Supreme Court did provisionally release van Roosmalen from prison last month [August 2007].

The Rights and Wrongs

However, van Roosmalen's case is more complex than it might initially appear. Firstly, he has faced charges of "improper appropriation" relating to the decision to offer sponsors the opportunity to have their name attached to newly discovered species—a practice which, although widely adopted in the past, now raises eyebrows in the research community itself.

And it is clear that under Brazilian law, van Roosmalen should have sought permission to capture and keep some of the animals he used for research. His frustration at the lengthy procedure this involves is understandable, but without permission, his experiments were illegal.

But it is widely believed that many other, equally frustrated, scientists collect samples without authorisation and without facing legal action. Indeed, some of van Roosmalen's supporters blamed his conviction on his high profile clashes with politically-influential landowners over campaigns to save the Amazonian rainforest, rather than regulators' zeal to protect local biodiversity.

Whether or not there has been undue political influence, it is clear that regulators in Brazil and elsewhere do not get the financial and human resources needed to carry out their tasks efficiently. The most obvious result has been the long delays in granting permissions for experiments, which has left all sides frustrated.

Arguing It Out

Scientists can legitimately argue that delays are costly for their research, and that they themselves could usefully contribute to formulating national policies, laws and regulations that implement CBD commitments.

But when they defend their own interests in the name of freedom for scientific inquiry, their case is weakened by the misdeeds of their predecessors, and occasionally their peers, whose abuse of such freedoms contributed to the current situation.

Scientists and conservationists alike . . . must remember that they share a common long-term interest in sensibly designed and effectively implemented mechanisms that protect biodiversity.

Conservationists also have a case when they defend the CBD, and the regulations flowing from it, as essential weapons in the fight to conserve native fauna and flora. But claims on who rightfully 'owns' this material are often more complex than activists acknowledge. Activists also need to acknowledge that a healthy science base is essential to their own cause.

Avoiding Lose-Lose Situations

Fortunately, the situation has improved significantly since the mid-1990s when, after the CBD was signed, there was a virtual freeze on collaboration between biologists in developed countries and those in countries such as Brazil. Careful negotiation has led to effective guidelines—for example on sharing samples—that show accommodation is possible.

But tensions and distrust remain high, as the intense feelings aroused by the van Roosmalen affair demonstrate. So scientists and conservationists alike, particularly the more 'activist' of the latter, must remember that they share a common long-term interest in sensibly designed and effectively implemented mechanisms that protect biodiversity.

Nobody wins when regulations are either ignored or over-zealously applied, whatever the supposed justification.

12

A Focus on At-Risk Biodiverse Regions Will Reduce Biodiversity Loss

Yasemin Erboy

Yasemin Erboy came to New York from Izmir, Turkey. She wrote this article while studying environmental science at Columbia University. She entered the graduate program in environmental management at Yale in September 2009.

Protecting biodiversity hotspots, areas rich in biodiversity that face serious threats, is one of the most effective ways to reduce biodiversity loss. These hotspots contain large numbers of species that are specific to a small percentage of the Earth's land surface. Making conservation budget decisions based on a species' threat of extinction and its tendency to be found in only one place makes sense. Because the knowledge about biodiversity hotspots is constantly growing, preemptive protection of at-risk areas also is important. In addition, environmental policy makers should establish protected areas that recognize the Earth is a dynamic system and that acknowledge that habitats may shift as the climate changes.

One day, as I wandered aimlessly from one Internet site to another, I came across the Web site of Conservation International [CI], a group dedicated to the conservation of thousands of species that are on the brink of extinction. As we all know, unsustainable living is having such a detrimental effect on wildlife that [it] is hovering on the edge of irreparable destruction, enhancing the natural extinction process to such an extent that we might be facing a mass extinction like the one that killed the dinosaurs.

Identifying Biodiversity Hotspots

What I did not know, however, was the concept of "hotspots" that CI has implemented and the consequent awareness and protection of wildlife it has achieved. As described on its Web site, these "biodiversity hotspots" are home to huge numbers of endemic species, yet their combined area of remaining habitat covers only 2.3 percent of the Earth's land surface. Each hotspot faces extreme threats, having lost at least 70 percent of its original natural vegetation. To put this into context, over 50 percent of the world's plant species and 42 percent of all terrestrial vertebrate species are endemic to the 34 biodiversity hotspots, and if they are not protected effectively and immediately, they will be lost.

Because conservation budgets are insufficient given the number of species threatened with extinction, endemism, or "the degree to which species are found solely in a given place," plays a crucial role in decision-making and prioritizing which areas to conserve first. The higher the degree of endemism of a hotspot, the more irreplaceable it is. The more irreplaceable it is, the more costly it is to conserve it. Here the problem arises—stopping anthropogenic species extinctions is weighed against limited conservation resources. Ideally endemism would win, but integrating cost and opportunity into a web of conservation priorities and threats is not easy. With time, threats to them and their impacts change, and our understanding of them is continually improving. This is why, as CI argues, we "need a dual conservation strategy that always prioritizes endemic-rich areas and ensures that we protect the most threatened places, while preemptively protecting equally unique places that are not yet under extreme threat." This "double-edged sword" is essential if we are to maximize the protection and prosperity of these fast-dwindling hotspots. Focusing most of the efforts on areas both under extreme threat and housing the most variety of species, while at the same time leaving enough energy to protect potentially threatened areas so the work does not continue in an endless loop is a lot of balls to juggle—yet CI seems to be successfully doing so.

Species' habitats fluctuate and shift as climate conditions change, and defining and protecting [biodiversity] hotspots is an active problem.

Focusing on Hotspots

Thus efforts must be focused on threatened biodiversity hotspots and high-biodiversity wilderness areas, which are irreplaceable but still largely intact—this is why CI's work is both so effective and so crucial to maintaining the ecological diversity of the planet. It is reassuring to know that this is not a lone effort on CI's part, but that the world is catching up on the importance of conserving these hotspots. According to the CI Web site, more than $750 million has been invested in saving such hotspots in the past 15 years—"perhaps the largest financial investment in any single conservation strategy." This sounds like a definite solution to the problem at hand—yet as a rather cynical environmental activist, I cannot help asking myself how these investments are actually put to use in a world where habitat destruction and deforestation, ceaseless anthropogenic climate change, and genetic engineering is leading to a soon-to-be irreversible mass extinction. Introduction of exotic plant species into hotspots, increasing numbers of predatory species, and direct exploitation of species for food, medicine, and trade are all growing and ceaseless threats. Combined with the detrimental effects of global warming and climate fluctuations, they do not leave much room for a significant improvement unless the investments have the highest priority on everyone's agenda and are implemented in the most effective strategy possible. As another environmental sciences major, Ilana Somasunderam, CC '09 [Columbia College, a residential college within Columbia University, Class of 2009], puts it: "perhaps the government of the U.S., a country whose unsustainable lifestyle is greatly contributing to the biodiversity issue, should make this a priority. Sure, they throw a few million dollars here and another couple million dollars there, but when you think of the money that's being spent on the war in Iraq (which amounts to about $200 million a day) it just seems like nothing is being done about this problem on a governmental level."

Our initial response must therefore be the establishment and effective management of protected areas—feasible since the total area in question is insignificant compared to the importance of the life it contains. It should, on principle, be possible to protect these areas and exchange a small fraction of our material gain from them for the continuation of the ecological diversity crucial to the functioning of the planet that we also inhabit. We must focus on making sure that such habitats will be protected and taken care of in the long term, as more endangered habitats are added. This is not so straightforward, since our planet is a dynamic system whose workings are changing—species' habitats fluctuate and shift as climate conditions change, and defining and protecting such hotspots is an active problem. Our response must not only focus on the present needs of hotspots, but also make preparations for future habitats in danger, and hope that everyone realizes its importance before it is too late. In short, we need to follow the footsteps that CI has taken and lend our support to this workable and optimally efficient strategy.

13

Religious Leaders Should Be Concerned About Biodiversity

Edward O. Wilson

Edward O. Wilson is a highly respected authority on biodiversity and the evolution of social behavior. He is an emeritus professor at Pellegrino University, honorary curator in Entomology at Harvard University, Pulitzer-prize winning author, and the 1999 Humanist of the Year.

The following excerpt is from an imagined letter to a Southern Baptist pastor about the necessity for an alliance between science and religion to save the Earth's biodiversity. While a scientist and a Southern Baptist pastor may have fundamental ideological differences, the defense of the Creation is a universal value that serves all humanity. While some Christians believe that the fate of non-human life forms does not matter, surely people of different ideologies might agree that protecting biodiversity will improve life for humanity. Indeed, the risks of ignoring the threats to biodiversity are grave. The unintended consequences of species loss, such as disease and famine, are not often known until it is too late. There is hope, but the only way to save biodiversity is for scientists and religious leaders to work together to preserve the Earth—the Creation.

D ear Pastor:

We have not met, yet I feel I know you well enough to call you friend. First of all, we grew up in the same faith. As a boy

I too answered the altar call; I went under the water. Although I no longer belong to that faith, I am confident that if we met and spoke privately of our deepest beliefs, it would be in a spirit of mutual respect and good will. I know we share many precepts of moral behavior. Perhaps it also matters that we are both Americans and, insofar as it might still affect civility and good manners, we are both Southerners.

Fundamental Differences

I write to you now for your counsel and help. Of course, in doing so, I see no way to avoid the fundamental differences in our respective worldviews. You are a literalist interpreter of Christian Holy Scripture. You reject the conclusion of science that mankind evolved from lower forms. You believe that each person's soul is immortal, making this planet a way station to a second, eternal life. Salvation is assured those who are redeemed in Christ.

I am a secular humanist. I think existence is what we make of it as individuals. There is no guarantee of life after death, and heaven and hell are what we create for ourselves, on this planet. There is no other home. Humanity originated here by evolution from lower forms over millions of years. And yes, I will speak plain, our ancestors were apelike animals. The human species has adapted physically and mentally to life on Earth and no place else. Ethics is the code of behavior we share on the basis of reason, law, honor, and an inborn sense of decency, even as some ascribe it to God's will.

The defense of living Nature is a universal value.

For you, the glory of an unseen divinity; for me, the glory of the universe revealed at last. For you, the belief in God made flesh to save mankind; for me, the belief in Promethean fire seized to set men free. You have found your final truth; I am still searching. I may be wrong, you may be wrong. We may both be partly right.

Does this difference in worldview separate us in all things? It does not. You and I and every other human being strive for the same imperatives of security, freedom of choice, personal dignity, and a cause to believe in that is larger than ourselves.

Setting Aside Differences

Let us see, then, if we can, and you are willing, to meet on the near side of metaphysics in order to deal with the real world we share. I put it this way because you have the power to help solve a great problem about which I care deeply. I hope you have the same concern. I suggest that we set aside our differences in order to save the Creation. The defense of living Nature is a universal value. It doesn't rise from, nor does it promote, any religious or ideological dogma. Rather, it serves without discrimination the interests of all humanity.

Pastor, we need your help. The Creation—living Nature—is in deep trouble. Scientists estimate that if habitat conversion and other destructive human activities continue at their present rates, half the species of plants and animals on Earth could be either gone or at least fated for early extinction by the end of the century. A full quarter will drop to this level during the next half century as a result of climate change alone. The ongoing extinction rate is calculated in the most conservative estimates to be about a hundred times above that prevailing before humans appeared on Earth, and it is expected to rise to at least a thousand times greater or more in the next few decades. If this rise continues unabated, the cost to humanity, in wealth, environmental security, and quality of life, will be catastrophic.

Surely we can agree that each species, however inconspicuous and humble it may seem to us at this moment, is a masterpiece of biology, and well worth saving. Each species possesses a unique combination of genetic traits that fits it more or less precisely to a particular part of the environment. Prudence alone dictates that we act quickly to prevent the extinction of species and, with it, the pauperization of Earth's ecosystems—hence of the Creation.

Uniting Religion and Science

You may well ask at this point, Why me? Because religion and science are the two most powerful forces in the world today, including especially the United States. If religion and science could be united on the common ground of biological conservation, the problem would soon be solved. If there is any moral precept shared by people of all beliefs, it is that we owe ourselves and future generations a beautiful, rich, and healthful environment.

I am puzzled that so many religious leaders, who spiritually represent a large majority of people around the world, have hesitated to make protection of the Creation an important part of their magisterium. Do they believe that human-centered ethics and preparation for the afterlife are the only things that matter? Even more perplexing is the widespread conviction among Christians that the Second Coming is imminent, and that therefore the condition of the planet is of little consequence. Sixty percent of Americans, according to a 2004 poll, believe that the prophecies of the book of Revelation are accurate. Many of these, numbering in the millions, think the End of Time will occur within the life span of those now living. Jesus will return to Earth, and those redeemed by Christian faith will be transported bodily to heaven, while those left behind will struggle through severe hard times and, when they die, suffer eternal damnation. The condemned will remain in hell, like those already consigned in the generations before them, for a trillion trillion years, enough for the universe to expand to its own, entropic death, time enough for countless universes like it afterward to be born, expand, and likewise die away. And that is just the beginning of how long condemned souls will suffer in hell—all for a mistake they made in choice of religion during the infinitesimally small time they inhabited Earth.

For those who believe this form of Christianity, the fate of ten million other life forms indeed does not matter. This and other similar doctrines are not gospels of hope and compassion. They are gospels of cruelty and despair. They were not born of the heart of Christianity. Pastor, tell me I am wrong!

An Alternative Ethic

However you will respond, let me here venture an alternative ethic. The great challenge of the twenty-first century is to raise people everywhere to a decent standard of living while preserving as much of the rest of life as possible. Science has provided this part of the argument for the ethic: The more we learn about the biosphere, the more complex and beautiful it turns out to be. Knowledge of it is a magic well: The more you draw from it, the more there is to draw. Earth, and especially the razor-thin film of life enveloping it, is our home, our wellspring, our physical and much of our spiritual sustenance.

I know that science and environmentalism are linked in the minds of many with evolution, Darwin, and secularism. Let me postpone disentangling all this . . . and stress again: To protect the beauty of Earth and of its prodigious variety of life forms should be a common goal, regardless of differences in our metaphysical beliefs.

To make the point in good gospel manner, let me tell the story of a young man, newly trained for the ministry, and so fixed in his Christian faith that he referred all questions of morality to readings from the Bible. When he visited the cathedral-like Atlantic rainforest of Brazil, he saw the manifest hand of God and in his notebook wrote, "It is not possible to give an adequate idea of the higher feelings of wonder, admiration, and devotion which fill and elevate the mind."

That was Charles Darwin in 1832, early into the voyage of *HMS Beagle*, before he had given any thought to evolution.

I am heartened by the movement growing within Christian denominations to support global conservation.

And here is Darwin, concluding *On the Origin of Species* in 1859, having first abandoned Christian dogma and then, with his newfound intellectual freedom, formulated the theory of evolution by natural selection: "There is grandeur in this view of life, with its several powers, having been originally breathed into a few forms or into one; and that, whilst this planet has gone cycling on according to the fixed law of gravity, from so simple a beginning endless forms most beautiful and most wonderful have been, and are being, evolved."

Darwin's reverence for life remained the same as he crossed the seismic divide that divided his spiritual life. And so it can be for the divide that today separates scientific humanism from mainstream religion. And separates you and me.

You are well prepared to present the theological and moral arguments for saving the Creation. I am heartened by the movement growing within Christian denominations to support global conservation. The stream of thought has arisen from many sources, from evangelical to Unitarian. Today it is but a rivulet. Tomorrow it will be a flood.

I already know much of the religious argument on behalf of the Creation, and would like to learn more. I will now lay before you and others who may wish to hear it the scientific argument. You will not agree with all that I say about the origins of life—science and religion do not easily mix in such matters—but I like to think that in this one life-and-death issue we have a common purpose.

The Risks of Denial

Dear Pastor, what I fear most is the pervasive combination of religious and secular ideology of a kind that sees little or no harm in the destruction of the Creation.

A cheerful faith in human destiny dismisses the rest of life through successive denials. The first says, Why worry? Extinction is natural. Life forms have been dying out over billions of years of history without any clear harm to the biosphere. New species are constantly being born to replace them.

All this is true as far as it goes, but with a terrible twist. Except for giant meteorite strikes or other catastrophes every 100 million years or so, Earth has never experienced anything like the contemporary human juggernaut. With the global species extinction rate now exceeding the global species birthrate at least a hundredfold, and soon to increase to ten times that much, and with the birthrate falling through the loss of sites where evolution can occur, the number of species is plummeting. The original level of biodiversity is not likely to be regained in any period of time that has meaning for the human mind.

The second stage of denial takes form in a question, Why do we need so many species anyway? Why care, especially when the vast majority are bugs, weeds, and fungi?

It is easy to look past these creepy-crawlers, forgetting that only a century ago, before the rise of the modern conservation movement, native birds and mammals were eliminated with equal disregard. In just four decades, the population of passenger pigeons plunged from hundreds of millions to zero.

People today understand what was lost or almost lost in these cases by the unintended consequences of human greed. In time they will come similarly to value other creatures that still fall below their notice.

People will more widely share the knowledge acquired by biologists that these often obscure life forms run Earth completely free for us. Each is a masterpiece of evolution, exquisitely well adapted to the niches of the natural environment in which it occurs. The surviving species around us are thousands to millions of years old. Their genes, having been tested each generation in the crucible of natural selection, are codes written by countless episodes of birth and death. Their careless erasure is a tragedy that will haunt human memory forever.

Even if that much is granted, the third stage of denial predictably emerges: Why rush to save all of biodiversity now? We have more important things to do. Priority is owed economic growth, jobs, military defense, democratic expansion, alleviation of poverty, medicine. Why not collect or gather live specimens of every species, and breed them in zoos, aquaria, and botanical gardens, for later return to the wild? Yes, this rescue operation is available as a last resort, and has in fact saved a few plants and animals that were on the brink of extinction.

With the smaller population . . . and a higher and sustainable per capita consumption spread more evenly around the world, this planet can be paradise.

The sobering truth is that all the zoos in the world can sustain breeding populations of a maximum of only two thousand mammal species, out of about five thousand known to exist. A similar limitation exists for birds. Botanical gardens and arboreta are more capacious, but would be overwhelmed by the tens of thousands of plant species needing protection. The same is true of fishes that might be saved in aquaria. A lot of good can be accomplished, but at considerable expense per species, and it can only make a dent in the problem.

A Planetary Ark

There is no solution available, I assure you, to save Earth's biodiversity other than the preservation of natural environments in reserves large enough to maintain wild populations sustainably. Only Nature can serve as the planetary ark.

So here, Pastor, is a homily of my own I offer to counter that of the exemptionalist:

Save the Creation, save all of it! No lesser goal is defensible. However biodiversity arose, it was not put on this planet to be erased by any one species. This is not the time, nor will there ever be a time, when circumstance justifies destroying Earth's natural heritage. Proud though we are of our special status, and justifiably so, let us keep our world-changing capabilities in perspective. All that human beings can imagine, all the fantasies we can conjure, all our games, simulations, epics, myths, and histories, and, yes, all our science dwindle to little beside the full productions of the biosphere. We have not even discovered more than a small fraction of Earth's life forms. We understand fully no one species among the millions that have survived our onslaught.

Think of it. With the smaller population that can be reached within a century, and a higher and sustainable per capita consumption spread more evenly around the world, this planet can be paradise. But only if we also take the rest of life with us.

Organizations to Contact

The editors have compiled the following list of organizations concerned with the issues debated in this book. The descriptions are derived from materials provided by the organizations. All have publications or information available for interested readers. The list was compiled on the date of publication of the present volume; the information provided here may change. Readers need to remember that many organizations take several weeks or longer to respond to inquiries.

American Council on Science and Health (ACSH)

1995 Broadway, 2nd Floor, New York, NY   10023-5860
(212) 362-7044 • fax: (212) 362-4919
e-mail: acsh@acsh.org
Web site: www.acsh.org

ACSH is a consumer education consortium concerned with environmental and health-related issues. The council publishes the quarterly *Priorities*, position papers, and articles such as "Why Biodiversity Is a Public Health Issue" and "Problems with the Cartagena Protocol," which are available on its Web site.

Cato Institute

1000 Massachusetts Ave. NW, Washington, DC   20001-5403
(202) 842-0200 • fax: (202) 842-3490
e-mail: cato@cato.org
Web site: www.cato.org

The Cato Institute is a libertarian public policy research foundation that aims to limit the role of government and to protect civil liberties. In addition to a wide range of journals and newsletters, Cato publishes books, including *Meltdown: The Predictable Distortion of Global Warming by Scientists, Politi-*

cians, and the Media. Publications offered on its Web site include recent issues of the bimonthly *Cato Policy Report*, the quarterly journal *Regulation*, policy studies, and opinions and commentary.

Conservation International
2011 Crystal Dr., Suite 500, Arlington, VA   22202
(703) 341-2400
Web site: www.conservation.org

Conservation International's goal is to promote biological research and work with national governments and businesses to protect biodiversity hot spots worldwide. On its Web site, the organization publishes fact sheets that explain its values, mission, and strategies, as well as news and reports of its successes.

Earth Island Institute (EII)
300 Broadway, Suite 28, San Francisco, CA   94133-3312
(415) 788-3666 • fax: (415) 788-7324
Web site: www.earthisland.org

Founded in 1982 by veteran environmentalist David Brower, EII develops and supports projects that counteract threats to the biological and cultural diversity that sustain the environment. Through education and activism, EII promotes the conservation, preservation, and restoration of the Earth. It publishes the quarterly, *Earth Island Journal.*

Environment Canada
351 St. Joseph Blvd., Place Vincent Massey, 8th Floor
Gatineau, Quebec   K1A 0H3
(819) 997-2800 • fax: (819) 994-1412
e-mail: enviroinfo@ec.gc.ca
Web site: www.ec.gc.ca

Environment Canada is a department of the Canadian government. Its goal is the achievement of sustainable development in Canada through conservation and environmental protection. The department publishes reports, fact sheets, news, and speeches, many of which are available on its Web site.

Environmental Defense Fund

257 Park Ave. S, New York, NY   10010
(212) 505-2100
Web site: www.environmentaldefense.org

Founded by scientists in 1967, the Environmental Defense Fund conducts original research or enlists outside experts to solve environmental problems. The advocacy group forms partnerships with corporations to promote environmentally friendly business practices. On its Web site, the fund publishes news, fact sheets, reports, and articles, including "The Importance of Wildlife and the Diversity of Life" and "Climate Change Could Be a Leading Cause of Biodiversity Loss."

Friends of the Earth

1717 Massachusetts Ave. NW, Suite 600
Washington, DC   20036-2002
(877) 843-8687 • fax: (202) 783-0444
e-mail: foe@foe.org
Web site: www.foe.org

Friends of the Earth is a national advocacy organization dedicated to protecting the planet from environmental degradation; preserving biological, cultural, and ethnic diversity; and empowering citizens to have an influential voice in decisions affecting the quality of their environment. It publishes the quarterly *Friends of the Earth* newsmagazine, which is available on its Web site, as well as fact sheets, news, articles, and reports on six environmental issue links.

Global Warming International Center (GWIC)

PO Box 50303, Palo Alto, CA   94303-0303
(630) 910-1551 • fax: (630) 910-1561
Web site: www.globalwarming.net

GWIC is an international body that provides information on global warming science and policy to industries and governmental and nongovernmental organizations. The center sponsors research supporting the understanding of global warming and ways to reduce the problem. It publishes the quarterly journal, *World Resource Review.*

Greenpeace USA

702 H St. NW, Washington, DC   20001
(800) 326-0959 • fax: (202) 462-4507
e-mail: info@wdc.greenpeace.org
Web site: www.greenpeaceusa.org

Greenpeace opposes nuclear energy and the use of toxic chemicals and it supports ocean and wildlife preservation. It uses controversial direct-action techniques and strives for media coverage of its actions in an effort to educate the public. The organization publishes the quarterly magazine *Greenpeace*, and it has published various books, including *Coastline* and *The Greenpeace Book on Antarctica.* On its Web site, Greenpeace publishes fact sheets, reports such as *Food Security and Climate Change: The Answer is Biodiversity*, and articles such as "How Should We Protect Biodiversity and Our Climate?"

Natural Capital Project

371 Serra Mall, Stanford University
Stanford, CA   94305-5020
fax: (650) 723-5920
e-mail: ccolvin@stanford.edu
Web site: www.naturalcapitalproject.org

The Natural Capital Project is a joint venture of Stanford University, the Nature Conservancy and the World Wildlife Fund that explores ecosystem services and economy incentives for preserving biodiversity. It develops tools to quantify the value of natural capital to integrate scientific and economic understanding of natural assets into land-use and investment decisions. Its Web site provides information on books by project members, such as *The New Economy of Nature: The Quest to Make Conservation Profitable*, and many articles by project members, including "Using Science to Assign Value to Nature" and "When Agendas Collide: Human Welfare and Biological Conservation."

Natural Resources Defense Council (NRDC)
40 W 20th St., New York, NY 10011
(212) 727-2700
e-mail: proinfo@nrdc.org
Web site: www.nrdc.org

NRDC is a nonprofit organization that uses both law and science to protect the planet's wildlife and wild places and to ensure a safe and healthy environment for all living things. NRDC publishes the quarterly magazine *OnEarth* and the bimonthly bulletin *Nature's Voice*. On its Web site NRDC provides links to specific environmental topics and news, articles, and reports, including *The Cost of Climate Change* and *Keeping Oceans Wild*.

Nature Conservancy
4245 N Fairfax Dr., Suite 100, Arlington, VA 22203-1606
(703) 841-5300
Web site: www.nature.org

Nature Conservancy supports land conservation to protect wildlife habitat in the United States and in more than thirty nations. It is the leading conservation organization working around the world to protect ecologically important lands and waters for nature and people. On its Web site, the conservancy posts fact sheets and news on its current initiatives, a blog, and articles published in its quarterly *Nature Conservancy* magazine.

Pew Center on Global Climate Change
2101 Wilson Blvd., Suite 550, Arlington, VA 22201
(703) 516-4146 • fax: (703) 841-1422
Web site: www.pewclimate.org

The Pew Center on Global Climate Change is a nonpartisan organization dedicated to educating the public and policy makers about the causes and potential consequences of global climate change and to informing them of ways to reduce the emissions of greenhouse gases. Its reports include *Designing a Climate-Friendly Energy Policy* and *The Science of Climate Change*.

Property and Environment Research Center (PERC)
2048 Analysis Dr., Suite A, Bozeman, MT 59718
(406) 587-9591
e-mail: perc@perc.org
Web site: www.perc.org

PERC is a nonprofit research and educational organization that seeks market-oriented solutions to environmental problems. The center holds a variety of conferences and provides educational material. It publishes the quarterly newsletter *PERC Reports*, commentaries, research studies, and policy papers, many of which are available on its Web site, including "Conserving Biodiversity through Markets: A Better Approach," "Meet the Enviropreneurs of 2008," and "Is there a Biodiversity Jackpot?"

Resources for the Future (RFF)
1616 P St. NW, Washington, DC 20036
(202) 328-5000
Web site: www.rff.org

Founded in 1952, RFF is a think tank that pioneered the application of economics as a tool to develop effective environmental policy. It conducts independent research on global warming and other environmental issues. RFF Press publishes books, reports, and issue briefs that reflect a broad range of approaches to the study of natural resources and the environment, including "What Is Biodiversity Worth? And to Whom?" It also publishes the quarterly *Resources* magazine, recent articles from which are available on its Web site, including "Biodiversity: What It Means, How It Works, and What the Current Issues Are."

Union of Concerned Scientists (UCS)
2 Brattle Sq., Cambridge, MA 02238
(617) 547-5552 • fax: (617) 864-9405
e-mail: ucs@ucsusa.org
Web site: www.ucsusa.org

UCS aims to advance responsible public policy in areas where science and technology play important roles. Its programs emphasize transportation reform, arms control, safe and renewable energy technologies, and sustainable agriculture. UCS publications include the twice-yearly magazine *Catalyst*, the quarterly newsletter *Earthwise*, and the electronic newsletter *Greentips*, recent issues of which are available on its Web site and which include articles on biodiversity. The union's Social Science Initiative link includes fact sheets on biodiversity and information on its Communicating Ecosystem Services (CES) program.

U.S. Environmental Protection Agency (EPA)

Ariel Rios Building, 1200 Pennsylvania Ave. NW
Washington, DC   20460
(202) 272-0167
Web site: www.epa.gov

The EPA is the federal agency in charge of protecting the environment and controlling pollution. The agency works toward these goals by enacting and enforcing regulations, identifying and fining polluters, assisting businesses and local environmental agencies, and cleaning up polluted sites. The EPA publishes speeches, testimony, periodic reports, and regional news on its Web site.

World Resources Institute (WRI)

10 G St. NE, Suite 800, Washington, DC   20002
(202) 729-7600 • fax: (202) 729-7610
Web site: www.wri.org

WRI conducts research on ecosystem threats and works with indigenous communities to balance human and wildlife needs. Its Web site provides links to its four primary areas of study: climate protection, governance, markets and enterprise, and people and ecosystems. WRI publishes fact sheets, working papers, and reports on its Web site, including "Biodiversity Loss: Cascade Effects" and "Measuring Nature's Benefits: A Preliminary Roadmap for Improving Ecosystem Service Indicators."

Worldwatch Institute

1776 Massachusetts Ave. NW, Washington, DC   20036-1904
(202) 452-1999 • fax: (202) 296-7365
e-mail: worldwatch@worldwatch.org
Web site: www.worldwatch.org

Worldwatch is a nonprofit public policy research organization dedicated to informing the public and policy makers about emerging global problems and trends and the complex links between the environment and the world economy. Its publications include *Vital Signs*, issued every year, the bimonthly magazine *World Watch*, the Environmental Alert series, and numerous policy papers and reports, including *Working for People and the Environment* and *Oceans in Peril: Protecting Marine Biodiversity*.

Bibliography

Books

Rosie Cooney and Barney Dickson, eds.   *Biodiversity and the Precautionary Principle.* Sterling, VA: Earthscan, 2005.

Gretchen C. Daily and Katherine Ellison   *The New Economy of Nature: The Quest to Make Conservation Profitable.* Washington, DC: Island Press, 2002.

Oliver Deke   *Environmental Policy Instruments for Conserving Global Biodiversity.* New York: Springer, 2008.

Robert G. Foottit and Peter H. Adler, eds.   *Insect Biodiversity: Science and Society.* Hoboken, NJ: Wiley-Blackwell, 2009.

L.L. Gaddy   *Biodiversity: Przewalski's Horse, Edna's Trillium, the Giant Squid, and Over 1.5 Million Other Species.* Lanham, MD: University Press of America, 2005.

Seymour Garte   *Where We Stand, A Surprising Look at the Real State of Our Planet.* New York: AMACON Books, 2007.

Dale D. Goble, J. Michael Scott, and Frank W. David, eds.   *Conserving Biodiversity in Human-Dominated Landscapes.* Washington, DC: Island Press, 2006.

Michael M. Gunter	*Building the Next Ark.* Lebanon, NH: Dartmouth College Press, 2004.
David L. Hawksworth and Alan T. Bull, eds.	*Human Exploitation and Biodiversity Conservation.* Dordrecht, Netherlands: Springer, 2006.
Michael I. Jeffery, Jeremy Firestone, and Karen Bubna-Litic, eds.	*Biodiversity Conservation, Law + Livelihoods: Bridging the North-South Divide.* New York: Cambridge University Press, 2008.
Bjørn Lomborg	*Cool It: The Skeptical Environmentalist's Guide to Global Warming.* London: Cyan, 2007.
Bjørn Lomborg	*The Skeptical Environmentalist, Measuring the Real State of the World.* New York: Cambridge University Press, 2001.
Thomas E. Lovejoy and Lee Hannah, eds.	*Climate Change and Biodiversity.* New Haven, CT: Yale University Press, 2005.
K.N. Ninan, ed.	*Conserving and Valuing Ecosystem Services and Biodiversity: Economic, Institutional and Social Challenges.* Sterling, VA: Earthscan, 2009.
Sahotra Sarkar	*Biodiversity and Environmental Philosophy: An Introduction.* New York: Cambridge University Press, 2005.
Edward O. Wilson	*The Creation, an Appeal to Save Life on Earth.* New York: W.W. Norton, 2006.

Edward O. Wilson *The Future of Life*. New York: Vintage, 2002.

David Zeigler *Understanding Biodiversity*. Westport, CT: Praeger, 2007.

Periodicals

Miguel A. Altieri "Poisoning the Planet," *Resurgence*, May-June 2009.

Michael Barker "Greenwashing Eden: The Uses and Abuses of Biodiversity," swans.com, June 1, 2009.

Aaron S. Bernstein and David S. Ludwig "The Importance of Biodiversity to Medicine," *Journal of the American Medical Association*, November 2008.

Chuck Burr "The Next Ten Years: What They Will Look Like," *Culture Change*, March 26, 2009.

Gedden Cascadia "A Few Too Many," *Earth First!*, May-June 2008.

Gerardo Ceballos and Paul R. Ehrlich "Global Mammal Distributions, Biodiversity Hotspots, and Conservation," *Proceedings of the National Academy of Sciences of the United States of America*, October 24, 2006.

Andrew A. Cunningham "A Walk on the Wild Side—Emerging Wildlife Diseases," *British Medical Journal*, 2005.

Sandra Diaz, Joseph Fargione, Stuart F. Chapin, and David Tilman — "Biodiversity Loss Threatens Human Well-Being," *PLoS Biology*, August 2005.

Michael K. Dorsey — "Future Markets in Biology: Life After Bioprospecting," *NACLA Report on the Americas*, March-April 2006.

Alister Doyle — "Biodiversity May Help Slow Disease Spread: Experts," *Reuters*, October 26, 2005.

Economist — "Fewer Creatures Great and Small; Biodiversity," October 18, 2008.

Michael Goulding and Adrian Forsyth — "Biodiversity in Jeopardy: There Are More Life Forms in Amazonia Than Anyplace Else. But by the End of This Century, There May Be Many Fewer," *American Prospect*, September 2007.

Cori Hayden — "Bioprospecting: The 'Promise' and Threat of the Market," *NACLA Report on the Americas*, March-April 2006.

Steven F. Hayward — "The United States and the Environment: Laggard or Leader?," *American Enterprise Online*, February 21, 2008.

Susan Hummel, Geoffrey H. Donovan, Thomas A. Spies, and Miles A. Hemstrom — "Conserving Biodiversity Using Risk Management: Hoax or Hope?" *Frontiers in Ecology and the Environment*, 2008.

Verlyn Klinkenborg
"How Will We Live Without Them?" *New York Times*, January 12, 2009.

Nancy Knowlton
"Marine Biodiversity in Jeopardy," *American Prospect*, December 2008.

Richard Land
"Interview: E.O. Wilson," *Religion & Ethics Newsweekly*, November 17, 2006.

Andrew May and David Smart
"Arable Farming and Biodiversity: Can the Two Coexist?," *Geography Review*, March 2006.

Russell A. Mittermeier and Thor Hanson
"Protecting Nature During War Can Help Recovery," *Huffington Post*, March 2, 2009.

John Moir
"So Many Species, So Little Time," *Orion*, January 1, 2009.

Norman Myers
"Biodiversity Hotspots Revisited," *Bioscience*, October 2003.

Michael Nelson and John Vucetich
"Abandon Hope," *Ecologist*, March 2009.

Sally Satel
"Diminishing Biodiverse Returns," *Tech Central Station*, February 16, 2005.

Science Daily
"Study Questions the 'Biodiversity Hotspot' Approach to Wildlife Conservation," December 12, 2006.

Emily Sohn
"Animal Biodiversity Keeps People Healthy," *Discovery.com*, May 19, 2009.

Will Steffan	"Looking Back to the Future," *Ambio*, November 2008.
Julia Whitty	"Gone: Mass Extinction and the Hazards of Earth's Vanishing Biodiversity," *Mother Jones*, May 1, 2007.
Edward O. Wilson	"Environment and the New Humanism," *Humanist*, November-December 2007.
Edward O. Wilson	"Protect Biodiversity Hot Spots and the Rest Will Follow," *Science News*, December 20, 2008.
Rachel Wynberg and Sarah Laird	"Bioprospecting: Tracking the Policy Debate," *Environment*, December 2007.

Index